An Easy Way to Become a Saint

An Easy Way to Become a Saint

FR. PAUL O'SULLIVAN, O.P.

TAN·BOOKS

CUM PERMISSU SUPERIORUM.

WITH ECCLESIASTICAL APPROBATION
June 13, 1949.

ISBN: 978-0-89555-398-0

Library of Congress Catalog Card No.: 90–70237

Published in the United States by
TAN Books
PO Box 269
Gastonia, NC 28053
www.TANBooks.com

Printed and bound in the United States of America

St. Therese the Little Flower at age 13.

Many think that it is practically impossible to be a saint—or at least extremely difficult.

In this book we offer our readers many easy but infallible means of reaching a high degree of sanctity.

PUBLISHER'S NOTE

An Easy Way to Become a Saint is one of the best-loved books of Fr. Paul O'Sullivan, O.P. All of Fr. O'Sullivan's works, in fact, have been favorites of Catholic readers for many years.

These books used to be published in Portugal, starting in the 1940's, and we found them to be very popular in the 1970's when we were importing them from there. In the meantime, however, the Portuguese publisher has ceased publishing these books, and St. Martin Apostolate in Dublin, a Dominican organization, has been distributing them.

We are very pleased to have been given permission to republish Fr. O'Sullivan's books. They are short, easy to understand and full of beautiful and encouraging stories from our Catholic heritage. They are conceived and written to help us live our Catholic Faith on an everyday basis in a full, rich, rewarding manner, so that we may reap both the happiness and peace in this world and the eternal salvation of our souls in the next that come from doing God's holy will.

Fr. O'Sullivan was obviously convinced that it was not so hard to become a saint—if we will only make use of the means Christ has put at our disposal in the Catholic Religion—and he has set out to show us the way.

We hope that *An Easy Way to Become a Saint* will be more popular than ever in this new edition. And we trust that it will help many to realize that holiness is truly within our reach, if we will take advantage of the many rich opportunities to gain graces which God sends us every single day.

—The Publishers
May 15, 1990

CONTENTS

An Easy Way to Become a Saint

These words will come as a surprise to many readers, but greater will be their surprise on perusing the following pages to see how true the words are.

1. To be a saint is to love God. Now what is easier than to love a God who is infinitely good and who loves us with infinite love?

Our hearts were made expressly to love Him, just as our eyes were made to see, our ears to hear. Surely there can be no difficulty in doing that for which we were expressly made.

2. To be a saint is to do all our actions for love of God. He made us to love and serve Him. He gave us our wonderful faculties to use for our own happiness and benefit, but He asks us to do all we do for love of Him. In return, He will give us a rich reward for our *every* action. This is what St. Paul tells us to do: "Whatever you do in word or work, do all in the name of the Lord Jesus Christ." (*Col.* 3:17).

Thus another infallible and easy way to become a saint is to do all we do for love of God.

3. God has given us a beautiful religion made especially for our poor human hearts, a religion of peace and love, a religion which gives us abundant helps to correct our faults and defects, a religion that gives strength to the weakest and

consoles the most broken-hearted. Those who practice this all-wise and consoling religion are truly saints.

The one difficulty in performing these three duties is not so much our weakness as our *lamentable ignorance*. We do not love God, simply because we do not know Him. We have been living with utterly erroneous ideas about Him. We look on God as a stern God, a God of majesty, whom we reverence, but fear; we only think of Him as a God of justice who punishes our sins. There we stop. That, as such, is a *caricature* of God, for God *above all* is a God of sweetness, mercy and love, a God who loves us most tenderly and desires our love in return.

We do not offer our actions for the love of God because we do not realize that our *every* thought, word and act give God pleasure and obtain for us great merit, if only we do them for love of Him. But because we do not realize this fact, the countless acts of the day, which might so easily bring us immense rewards, are utterly lost.

How imperfectly understood is our glorious Religion!

By many it is looked on as a hard duty that must be performed. They look on the Ten Commandments as restrictions to their liberty, instead of seeing them as they are—the surest guarantees of their happiness.

The treasures of joy and consolation which our Religion offers, the helps and strength it gives are little known. Prayer, instead of being a pleasure, is looked upon as a penance. The Sacraments, which are very rivers of grace, are little appreciated, little used. All this is owing to our *ignorance*. In a word, what we most need is an intelligent grasp of our divinely beautiful and all-wise Religion, one which will secure for us not only a high degree of holiness but the greatest possible measure of happiness.

The prevailing idea of many is that holiness implies leading a sad and austere life; whereas, true holiness gives us immense joy, consolation and strength.

Many too think that it is practically impossible to be a saint, or at least extremely difficult.

We offer our readers in this booklet many *easy* but *infallible* means of reaching a high degree of sanctity.

CHAPTER 1

Two Kinds of Saints

There are saints and saints. Some we may call "extraordinary saints" and some "ordinary saints."

Extraordinary saints are raised up by God for some extraordinary mission, and to these God gives extraordinary means to carry out that mission.

Such were, for instance, St. Dominic, St. Francis of Assisi, St. Ignatius Loyola and a host of others.

St. Dominic was raised up by God to defend the Church against the Albigensian heretics, who taught the vilest doctrines and perpetrated the most hideous crimes. Kings sent armies against them, the Pope sent holy men to check them, but all in vain.

God then raised up St. Dominic who, by the holiness of his life and his earnest preaching, converted 100,000 of these hardened sinners in a remarkably short time.

Notwithstanding his austere life and incessant labors, there was no one more joyful, more lovable than St. Dominic. He was sad only when he heard of the sorrows of others or of offenses committed against his dear Lord.

The Saint founded three religious orders, which have given to the Church notable saints, missionaries, martyrs, bishops and popes.

What especially endears him to us is the fact that it was he who gave us the Rosary, which God's Holy Mother had given to him.

Who has not heard of the seraphic St. Francis of Assisi, so famous for his profound humility, his extreme poverty and his burning love of God, as a reward of which he received on his hands and feet and in his side the Sacred Stigmata, the marks of Christ's five wounds.

He, too, founded three religious orders, which have given many and great saints to the Church, people such as St. Bonaventure, St. Anthony of Padua, St. Clare and many others, saints who shine as bright stars in the firmament of Heaven.

St. Ignatius of Loyola is another example of an extraordinary saint. He began life as a soldier in the army of Spain, but God called him to be a great soldier of Holy Church.

To him was given the mission to battle against the pseudo-reformers, as to St. Dominic had been given the task of converting the Albigenses.

His glorious order, the Society of Jesus, has done and is ever doing a mighty work for the glory of God and for the welfare of the world at large. His sons are ever in the vanguard of the battle, fighting valiantly against the enemies of Christ.

Now these extraordinary saints, inspired by God, used extraordinary means to achieve their great ends. They labored incessantly, spent long hours in prayer, fasted rigorously and did severe penance. God favored them with supernatural visions and revelations and gave them the power of working miracles.

Ordinary Christians are not called upon to do such mighty deeds, nor are they asked or advised to imitate the long prayers, the rigorous fasts of these extraordinary saints.

ORDINARY SAINTS

There is, however, a second class of saints, *ordinary saints*. Bear in mind that these saints are no less saints than the others; they are true saints and have reached exalted heights of sanctity, though in a different way.

They lead humble, simple lives, performing their daily duties well and using the ordinary but abundant means of sanctity given by God to all Christians.

These means we too can use, and by them we can attain a high degree of holiness.

Here is a good example of the ordinary saint.

THE TWO LADIES

The great St. Antony, the abbot who had spent long years in the desert, passing whole nights in prayer and performing severe penances, aware of how important the virtue of humility is in the spiritual life, asked God to make him profoundly humble.

In answer to his prayer, the Almighty directed him to visit two ladies in the neighboring city, who though simple and unpretentious in their manner of life, were, so God told Antony, holier than he who had spent long years in the practice of rigorous penance and unceasing prayer.

On entering their home, the Saint sought to discover the secret of such remarkable holiness; he asked them many questions as to the fasts they made, the length of their prayers, their austerities and the like, so that he might imitate them.

He was not a little surprised to learn that they did nothing exceptional. They observed the fasts of the Church; they said their prayers devoutly; they gave what little alms they could afford; they frequented the Sacraments, heard daily Mass and practiced the ordinary Christian virtues.

What impressed the Saint most was that they loved God very simply but very sincerely. God was the great reality in their lives. They did all their actions for love of Him. They performed their daily duties, seeing God in all they did. They accepted what happened to them, joys as well as sorrows, as coming directly from His hand.

That was all, but it sufficed to explain to the Saint the secret of their wonderful sanctity, *viz.*, they performed their duties well and they loved God.

There are thousands of such hidden, ordinary saints in the Church now, as there have been at all times.

SAINT THERESE OF LISIEUX

We have a striking example in our own days of a canonized saint who was actually given to us as an example of how to become holy, by what she herself tells us is the easy, the "little way" to Heaven.

St. Therese of Lisieux never worked a miracle, never enjoyed heavenly visions, never did anything extraordinary, but she did well all that she did. She tells us that she went to Heaven in an elevator (a lift).

In the Carmelite convent in which she lived, none of the sisters remarked anything wonderful in her conduct. She was sweet and joyful and was the sunshine of the community. Possibly some of the other sisters prayed longer and did more rigorous penances than she did.

An incident which took place before her death shows how simple and unpretentious was her life.

It was the custom in the convent for the prioress to write a short account of the life of each sister after that sister's death. During the illness of St. Therese, two sisters were heard speaking of this. One said to the other, "Poor Mother Prioress, whatever will she find to write about poor little Sister Therese?"

Yet this dear little saint began to work so many wonders after her death and obtain so many favors for those who had recourse to her that the whole *world* rang with her praises. She was solemnly canonized after a remarkably short time.

What a consolation she offers to those who wish to be holy! Hers was the little, the easy way, the elevator (lift) by which we, too, no matter how weak we are, can go to Heaven.

BENIGNA CONSOLATA

A second example that will encourage the humblest of us is the story of Benigna Consolata. Her life, her conduct were so ordinary that those who were most intimate with her had not the faintest idea that she was a saint.

She did not spend her nights in prayer, nor did she fast more rigorously than the others; she never worked miracles, yet her pure, humble life attracted the love of Our Lord, who frequently appeared to her and treated her with the most loving intimacy.

When speaking to her, He addressed her by her pet name, "Nina Mia." Her name was Benigna Philomena Consolata. He revealed to her the most consoling doctrines and said to her, "My dear little Secretary, write all I tell you, that others may know it."

The sisters who lived with her were utterly surprised when they learned after her death of her wonderful sanctity.

We ourselves may be surprised when we enter Heaven to see on high thrones those whom we knew on Earth but whose sanctity we did not suspect.

THE CHILDREN OF FATIMA

What happened more recently at Our Lady's sanctuary in Fatima will serve as another lesson on how to reach great holiness by simple means.

The Angel Guardian of Portugal came to prepare the three chosen children who were later on destined to see Our Blessed Lady.

Three things the Angel bade them do, *viz.*, to pray devoutly, to hate sin and to offer to God with patience the sufferings the Almighty would be pleased to send them, this for His greater glory and for the salvation of souls. God's Holy Mother herself, when she came, taught them the same lessons, which enabled these poor ignorant little children to become worthy of their glorious mission.

Can we not do what three poor, unlettered children did?

We ourselves from time to time meet with simple souls whose extraordinary virtue is made evident by a single act.

A dear old woman run over by a carriage in Dublin and horribly crushed was rushed to a hospital.

One of the Mercy Nuns who became her nurse tried with infinite delicacy to comfort and console her.

What was not the nun's surprise when the patient opened her eyes and said, "Sister dear, are you telling me to be resigned to God's holy will? Let me tell you that God's holy will has been always to me as welcome as the fruit to the tree."

Poor, with many sorrows and needs during her long life, she now, in the throes of agony, manifested her perfect union with the will of God.

Monsignor Robert Hugh Benson, the convert son of the Protestant Archbishop of Canterbury, while still a priest, went for a short visit to Catholic Ireland, of which he had heard so much.

At his request, a friend took him to visit some of the poor sick in their little homes.

He saw what he called *"wonders."* These dear sufferers amazed the young convert by their faith, patience and perfect resignation to the will of God.

One old man was suffering from an awful cancer, already in an advanced stage, which was eating away his breast.

Father Benson, full of compassion, tried to say some words of comfort to him.

"Oh my, Father, it's nothing," replied the old man. "Sure in a few days I will be with God in Heaven. Didn't He suffer much more for me?"

On his return to England, Father Benson wrote a touching article on the heroic patience and faith of these poor people. "They seem to see God," he said.

Owing to political troubles, an unfortunate man slew his enemy, a crown official.

Denounced by a perfidious friend of his own, he was arrested and condemned to death. He repented sincerely of his crime, but could not pardon his base accuser. The chaplain of the prison used his utmost efforts to induce him to go to Confession. "This I cannot do," he said, "because, though sorry for my crime, I cannot pardon my false friend. Thus my Confession would be bad."

A good Sister of Mercy won his heart by her "infinite" kindness and delicacy. She too tried to induce him to confess. In vain.

On the eve of his execution, she made a last, supreme effort. "Do you know who I am?" she asked him. "Yes, Sister, you are an Angel from Heaven."

"No, I am no Angel from Heaven, but I am the sister of the man whom you killed. I have pardoned you, I have fasted and prayed and done all I could to save your soul."

Amazed, the poor man fell on his knees and, in a flood of tears, kissed her feet.

"Yes, yes, Angel of God, for you are, indeed, an Angel. I forgive with all my heart my enemy, oh forgive me you."

Hers, indeed, was heroic forgiveness.

A single act, as we have said, reveals at times heroic sanctity.

The widow's alms won Our Lord's high approbation. "She has given more," He said, "than all the rest." She had given only a mite, but she gave it with all her heart.

The Good Thief's plea for mercy on the cross obtained plenary pardon for all his crimes.

The Publican's short prayer: "O God, have mercy on me, a sinner" made his soul as white as snow.

CHAPTER 2

How to Love God

Now let us see what we can do to become saints.

The first, the easiest and the most certain of all means to become a saint is to love God. We cannot possibly do anything holier, anything more pleasing to Him or anything more meritorious for ourselves.

We must learn all about the *Love of God*, for nothing is more important and more necessary for us, and nothing more conducive to our happiness.

To love God is *the great* work of our lives.

THE VALUE OF AN ACT OF LOVE

The value of one simple act of love is priceless. An act of love is of greater value than a thousand acts of any other virtue, just as one small diamond is worth more than a thousand gold pieces.

Our Blessed Lord told Benigna Consolata that any ordinary Christian can make an act of love in a moment which will have a reward for all eternity. We can make countless acts of love every day without any difficulty.

Secondly, He told her that one act of love gives Him more glory and more pleasure than a thousand horrible blasphemies give Him pain!

Thirdly, love wipes out our sins. One short act of love won for the Thief on the cross the promise that he would be that very day with Christ in Paradise.

On the other hand, all that we do which is not done for the love of God is worthless and will get no reward. We may toil for long years and receive great praise and honor for our labors, but if our work is not done for love of God, it is worthless.

Thus it is that a poor old woman who tells her beads at the church door, who bears her poverty patiently and who lives a quiet Christian life will have a higher place in Heaven than the great statesmen, the clever generals, the famous politicians, who direct the destinies of vast empires but who do not think of offering their work to God.

IS IT EASY TO LOVE GOD?

Most certainly, for God created us expressly to love Him and to love Him with all our hearts and souls. He is goodness itself. He has done everything to make us love Him. One might as well ask if it is easy for a child to love its mother, for a wife to love a dear husband, for a friend to love a friend, for a servant to love a good and generous master.

It is much easier to love God, who is infinitely good and sweet, God who loves us tenderly and affectionately, who is our dearest and most loving Father, our best, our truest Friend. All that is necessary is to realize His goodness.

The first great Commandment, the very essence of our holy Religion, is to *"Love God with all our heart and soul; with all our strength and mind."* This everyone must do.

Surely the all-merciful and wise God would never make the very first condition of His beautiful Religion something hard and difficult.

SOME SAY THAT THEY CANNOT LOVE GOD

There are people who say that they cannot love God. When they make an act of love and say, "Oh my God, I love You," they feel nothing in their hearts to correspond to their words. Their words sound hollow, cold and false. This is what they tell us themselves.

Unfortunately, this happens to many, and as a consequence, they are losing every day of their lives great merits and never experience the wonderful happiness they should enjoy in their Religion.

Why cannot they love God? There are four reasons:

First of all, they never ask God to help them to love Him.

Secondly, they do not realize, as we have said, what God is, His boundless goodness, His sweetness, mercy and love.

Thirdly, they do not understand how much He loves them.

Fourthly, they have no idea of all that He has done for them. All this we will now explain in detail.

Remark that when speaking of love we do not mean an emotional love, sentimental love; we speak of the solid love of God which comes from a clear, intelligent understanding of how good and sweet God is.

He Himself tells us: "Taste and see how sweet the Lord is," and again, "My yoke is sweet, My burden light."

HOW CAN WE ACQUIRE THE LOVE OF GOD?

First of all by prayer. Let us ask God every day and in every prayer we ever say to make us love Him. Let us offer every good act we do that He may give us this, the greatest of all graces, His blessed love.

In our morning prayers and evening prayers, in our Rosary, at Mass, in our Communions, let it be our first, our most earnest petition, *that we may love God*. Let us never say *any* prayer in which this is not our outstanding wish and intention.

Our Lord has promised over and over again and in the clearest terms to hear our prayers. He cannot break His word.

There is nothing that God gives us so willingly, so generously as His love. He wishes to give us this great grace even more than we wish to receive it. All we have to do is ask for it constantly.

It is certain that if we do this, our hearts, no matter how cold they may be, will gradually grow to love Him and that, too, with all their strength. They will overflow with love. They will love Him in the fullest sense of the word.

Have we never thought of this before? Why have we not asked God for this greatest of all gifts and graces? We ask so often for trivial favors and forget the most important of all. We should have been saints long ago had we done so.

Let us begin at once and ask God every day of our lives with *unbounded confidence for His holy love.*

The following incidents show how powerful prayer is in making us know and love God.

An American freethinker was eager to believe in God, but though he listened attentively to Cardinal Gibbons explaining the proofs of God's existence, he could not bring himself to believe. The Cardinal, seeing his good will, suggested that he should frequently say the following short prayer: "Oh, God, if You exist, make me know You."

This the freethinker did conscientiously for some time and received in return the gift of a lively and solid faith and with it the greatest happiness of his life.

Cardinal Newman had a similar experience. For many years he sought earnestly to discover the True Church by reading history, studying the works of the Fathers, discussing the subject with learned friends. In vain.

At last he exclaimed: "What have I been doing? I have sought by study and discussion to find the Truth, but I have not given sufficient time and attention to asking the gift of faith from God in prayer."

He at once changed his method and began to ask God earnestly to help him to find the True Church.

His prayers were speedily answered, and he not only saw the light himself but became a shining example to hundreds of others who, following his lead, joined the Catholic Church.

We too shall receive the gift and consolations of God's blessed love if we earnestly ask for it in our daily prayers.

Secondly, to love God we must know Him. Many people have a completely false notion of God. Though they *do not* say it in so many words, they think of God as a hard, a stern God, a God of justice who punishes sinners. Frequently, the teachers of the young are to blame for this. With the best intentions in the world they instill into the minds of their charges an exaggerated fear of the Almighty in order to deter them from sinning. But they do not teach them to *love* God.

The result is that boys and girls grow up and live all their lives with a false concept of God; they adore a false God, a God of fear.

It is true, the fear of God is the beginning of wisdom—but it must not be only a servile fear, but mainly the filial fear of children who grieve to offend and displease their parents. We too must fear to outrage our loving God, fear to crucify Him again and make a mockery of Him.

Hardened sinners, of course, who obstinately persist in offending God, know full well that their crimes deserve punishment. They have reason to fear.

But for the ordinary Christian, the all-engrossing concept of God must be clearly a God of infinite sweetness, mercy and love, a God of compassion, who wishes to lift us up and wipe away the stains of sin from our souls.

Above all, we must look on God as our most loving Father, our dearest Friend, a God in whom we have unbounded confidence, to whom we must go in all our troubles and whose help we can seek in all our needs.

We must serve God, not as servants, but as His dear children. We adore God, but with an adoration of love, like the Angels in Heaven, who are burning fires of love. The vision of God as He really is and as they see Him fills them with an ocean of joy and happiness.

Now this God, whom the Angels and Saints see in Heaven, is the same God whom we are asked to love. Did we see Him for one instant our souls would be so ravished with delight that they would tear themselves from our poor bodies and fly to Him.

Did the devil see God only for a moment, his whole being would be so inundated with happiness that never again could he feel the pains of Hell.

One may object: But we do not see God as the Angels do. That is true, but we know all about Him by our living faith, as surely as the Angels do by vision. We ought sometimes to place ourselves in spirit amidst the Angels and gaze on God, this especially when we are saying the *Gloria Patri*.

Soon, very soon, we shall see Him as they do, but for the moment let us use and *enjoy* our faith and thus anticipate the happiness of Heaven.

When one hears that he has inherited a great fortune, the news fills him at once with delight. He does not wait until the fortune is placed in his hands. Let us do likewise and begin to enjoy an anticipation of the immense, unbounded joys that await us in our Father's home.

GOD LOVES US

There is still something more thrilling that should fill us to overflowing with love for God, *viz.*, that God loves us with a personal, intimate, unbounded love. This glorious truth escapes many otherwise good Catholics. Either they do not know it or they do not grasp it. The certainty that the great God of Heaven and Earth loves me with a tender, affectionate love fills my soul with delight.

A husband finds immense happiness in the love of his dear wife. A friend prizes most highly the friendship of a true friend. Were a powerful prince or king to offer us his friendship and esteem, we should look on ourselves as very fortunate. But the Omnipotent God offers us His friendship and love, and we do not seem to accept it! What blindness, what appalling ignorance!

Our Lord offered Peter and John and Paul His love and friendship, and they accepted it. What happiness was not theirs! They became His great Apostles. He is offering it to us every day in the most pressing way. Why do we not accept it? What happiness are we not losing!

Let us *convince* ourselves that God is our dearest Friend, our most loving Father. Let us try to bring home to ourselves this wonderful truth. Has He not commanded us to call Him every day, "Our Father"? He means it. He asks for our love He does not wait to love us in Heaven; He loves us now on Earth and wishes to be loved in return by us.

IN A WORD

To love God is to be a saint, and the more we love God, the greater saints we shall be.

There is nothing easier than to love the God of infinite goodness and sweetness, the God who loves us with a personal, intimate, infinite love.

We shall most certainly love God if in all our prayers we ask Him for His blessed love.

If we know God, we must love Him. Therefore, we must do all we can to know God and fully to understand all the wonderful things that He has done for us.

CHAPTER 3

The Wonderful Things God Has Done for Us

OUR CREATION

God made us. How little we understand these words. Many have never heard a worthy explanation of them.

Who made us is one of the first questions in the Catechism. The brief answer is "God made us." Satisfied with these few words, Catholics go on living all their long lives hopelessly ignorant of the immense truth, joy and consolation hidden in them. As a result, they never even think of pouring out their most grateful thanks to the Almighty for this first infinite proof of love which He has given them.

They take the gift of their creation for granted and have not the faintest idea of how much they owe to God for bringing them out of nothing and giving them a glorious existence, an existence which will never cease.

Why did God create me? Simply because He loved me.

He saw me with all my poor weaknesses and defects. Yet He loved me that first moment with an infinite, personal love.

He could have just as easily created an Angel like St. Michael or a saint like St. Paul. But no, He created me, and since that moment He has never ceased loving me and will never cease to love me, unless I outrage and offend Him. Even then He will take me back to His friendship, if I repent and ask His pardon. We can understand the wonderful love a mother feels when her firstborn baby is placed in her arms. The love of all the mothers who ever lived is not equal to the tenderness and love of God when He holds us in His "arms."

He not only created us, but He created us from an infinite love.

How did He create us?

He created us with His own Divine hands. He did not depute an Angel to bring us into being, but employed in making us all His Omnipotent Power, His Divine Wisdom, His most tender love.

How perfect a thing we must be, and we do not know it!

All the famous painters, before beginning their great masterpieces, sought with the utmost diligence to find a suitable model so that their work might be perfect. Then they labored assiduously, using the minutest care in the execution of the picture. Almighty God, when creating us, also chose a model, the most perfect that even He could choose. That model was Himself. He made us to His own image and likeness! He made us like Himself!

Our likeness to God does not consist in a mere external resemblance, such as a photograph is of the person it represents. We are like to God in the very presence of our nature. Our souls are spiritual, like God; they are immortal, like God; they will live as long as God lives, for ever and for ever. They are beautiful, like God. How could they be otherwise since He, the Divine Artist, made them after the most perfect model.

We have two great faculties like those of God, our intellect and free will. He planted, too, in our inmost being, a craving for Him that nothing else can satisfy, so jealous is He of our love.

And for what destiny did He create us?

He made us for the highest destiny that was possible; He made us for Himself. He made us not to be His servants, but to be His own children, to be seated on thrones amidst the Angels, in His presence, sharing His infinite and eternal happiness.

How wonderful is the story of our creation! How is it possible that, knowing all this, we do not love God.

O, Dear Reader, think about and meditate on the infinite love of God in creating you. Weigh well every word that you have just read, for in every word you will find cause for joy and consolation.

THE GIFT OF DIVINE GRACE

Scarcely had we been born when our parents took us to the baptismal font. We had come into the world covered with a hideous leprosy, the filth and corruption of Original Sin, which we inherited from our First Parents.

The baptismal water was poured on our heads; we were bathed in the Precious Blood of Jesus, the same that was shed for us on Calvary.

These saving waters cleansed our souls from this hideous leprosy, leaving them as pure as the Angels in Heaven, while God, by an infinitely divine act of love, clothed our souls with a dazzling mantle taken from His own shoulders, *viz.*, with the robe of Divine Grace. This is a real participation in His own divine nature, as St. Peter assures us.

Did we see our soul clad in this divine mantle, we should be inclined to fall down and adore it. Nothing on this Earth can give us even a faint idea of a soul in Grace—an image of God, radiant, resplendent with divine beauty.

This divine grace is not only a *robe* of beauty, it is a *divine force*, a *new life*, which raises up our natures, giving them a new dignity. It penetrates into our faculties, illuminates our intellects and strengthens our will.

With it we can see and do what would be otherwise utterly impossible to our poor human nature.

How little do we understand the wonders God has done for us!

Foolish, ignorant parents are so blind that they sometimes leave their children for days without Baptism. The life of the newly born babe is so fragile that it may die at any moment, and then! That dear soul will never see God, through the culpable neglect of those who should love it most.

And even if the child does not die, why leave it wallowing in the corruption and filth of Original Sin?

Fathers and mothers strive to save their children from the least bodily defect, yet owing to cross ignorance, they allow them to remain so long under the curse and malediction of sin. Sad, woeful ignorance!

GOD WATCHES OVER US

Nothing perhaps manifests so clearly God's personal love for *each one* of us as His Divine Providence, which is watching over us every moment and in every event of our lives.

God has never taken His eyes off us since the moment of our creation, but is ever watching over us with loving care. Nothing happens to us that He does not see and permit. Not even a hair falls from our heads without His consent. Every moment of our lives is a new creation; our preservation is, as it were, a continual series of creations. Did God forget us or take His hand off us for a single moment, we should not only die, but fall back into our former nothingness. He takes care of the beasts that roam in the forests, of the little birds that fly in the air, He clothes the lilies of the field in a garb more beautiful than that of Solomon in all his glory. He sees every movement of the little fishes in the ocean, of the insects which are hidden in the earth. With far greater reason, He tells us, does He watch over us who are His dear children, so that all that happens to us is for our welfare and happiness, as St. Paul tells us: "All things work together unto good." (*Rom.* 8:28).

Nothing is so touching as the care a mother takes of her little one who is playing at her side. She is apparently intent on her sewing or knitting, but not for an instant does she lose sight of the child. At the first sign of danger, throwing aside what she has in hand, she rushes toward the little one and snatches it from the peril that threatened it.

This is exactly how God watches over us. His eyes are ever on us. Though we may think that our troubles come from an enemy or from some other cause or by chance, we may be sure that nothing happens to us that God does not will.

What is lacking is our want of confidence. If we only ran to God in all our troubles, our lot in life would be very different from what it is, very much happier.

OUR ANGEL GUARDIAN

One of the most marvelous dispensations of God's Providence is the fact that He has given to each one of us a special Angel to watch over us.

At the moment of our birth God calls one of His glorious Princes, one of His mighty Angels, and bids this Angel guard and guide, defend and protect us.

From that moment, this mighty Angel gives us all his loving care. He never leaves us, night or day. His duty after loving God is to love us. He devotes all his intelligence, all his strength, all his care to shield us from hurt and harm.

We can form no idea of the evils and dangers he saves us from, the countless great favors he has done us and is doing us every day.

Not content to use all his own power to help us, he is constantly praying for us to God.

Reading the story of St. Raphael in the Sacred Scriptures, we marvel at the infinite goodness of God in sending this great Angel to accompany the young Tobias on his long journey. The Angel proved to be a trusty friend. He not only accompanied him on his journey, protecting him from every danger, but he also obtained for him a most happy marriage and abundant wealth. He brought him home safely, to the delight of his parents, who were anxiously awaiting his return. As a final gift, he cured Tobias's old father, who had been blind.

Before leaving the now happy family, he revealed himself to them as one of the seven great Angels who stand before the throne of God and bade them bless and thank the Good God who had sent him to them.

This is certainly one of the most consoling and wonderful stories in the Bible, revealing to us the infinite sweetness and goodness of God.

Yet each one of us has a glorious Prince of Heaven with us, not for weeks or months but for all the long years of our lives, loving us most affectionately, defending us from countless evils and snatching us from dangers that we do not even see.

This dear Angel came to us at the moment of our birth and has been with us ever since. He will console us in Purgatory if we go there and will then accompany us to Heaven, where he will be with us forever and forever.

We marvel when reading this story of Raphael, but it is a much greater marvel that we have a glorious Angel ever at our sides and yet know and love him so little.

Have we ever even thanked God for this astounding proof of His goodness?

The culpable neglect of our dear Angel is one of the most lamentable and shameful faults of our life.

Read, Dear Reader, without fail, the beautiful book, *All About the Angels*, by E. D. M. [The pen name of Fr. Paul O'Sullivan, O.P.—Ed.]

CHAPTER 4

God's Greatest Proof of Love

THE INCARNATION

God, as St. Paul tells us, has poured out all the treasures of His infinite love for us in the mystery of the Incarnation. "What could I do for My vineyard that I have not done." Even God could do no more, could give no greater, no clearer, no proof of love more manifest than by becoming man for us.

He, the Omnipotent Creator, the God whom the Angels adore in Heaven, became a little babe, passed nine months in His Mother's womb, was born in a stable between two animals, lived for 30 years a hidden life—poor, humble and despised.

This was followed by three years of public life in which He did all that God could do to win our love.

Finally, He suffered a most ignominious and cruel death. Yet all these divine efforts to make us love Him are nullified by our incredible lack of appreciation.

Let us try to repair this hateful ingratitude by carefully pondering on the touching events in Our Lord's life. Let us try to rouse ourselves from this fatal lethargy, this insane want of appreciation of God's mercies and love.

We cannot say in truth that we have not seen God, for He became man expressly to show Himself to us. He remained on Earth 33 years that we might know Him as He is, that we might see for ourselves His infinite goodness, sweetness and love and thus be drawn and compelled to love Him in return. We are in one way more privileged than the Angels themselves, for God never became an Angel; He never took the Angelic Nature; He never raised it up to the dignity of the Godhead, as He did our human nature.

He remained on Earth 33 years, and His life can be summarized in these few words: *"He went about doing good to all."* He consoled the sorrowful and cured the sick, the lame, the blind, the deaf and the dumb.

He cleansed the poor lepers and brought them back to their homes, from which they had been driven. He raised the dead to life. What a story of love!

The multitudes thronged around Him, gazing on His Divine Face in raptures of joy, listening spell-bound to His words. One poor woman, speaking for all, cried out: "Blessed is the womb that bore Thee and the breasts that gave Thee suck!"

What an outburst of admiration! With good reason God's priests repeat every day in their Divine Office these beautiful words.

The crowds followed Him for long hours, even for entire days at a time, listening to Him, loving Him, charmed by His unceasing proofs of love and pity.

Seeing a poor widow weeping bitterly over her dead son, He was filled with pity and raised the boy to life and gave him back to his sorrowing mother.

He assisted at a wedding feast, and when the wine went short, He worked His first miracle and turned water into wine, lest the young couple might suffer shame!

How tenderly He showed His love for Peter, asking him three times, "Lovest thou me more than these? . . . Lovest thou me?" (*Jn.* 21:15, 16, 17).

At the Last Supper He allowed John to recline his head on His Divine Bosom. What ineffable love! John never did anything that pleased Jesus so much. What, indeed, could be more affectionate, more tender!

He loved to visit Martha and Mary in their home at Bethania, and when their brother Lazarus died, He, the *Son of God*, wept over His dear friend. Seeing the sorrow of Martha and Magdalen, He raised their brother to life, though he had been dead for four days.

All His life was one long series of these wonderful proofs of affection and love. The more we read the wonderful story of Jesus, the more we must love Him. We read stories of great men, of heroes, of heroines of charity and feel thrilled at what they have done, wishing only that we could do likewise.

What romance, what human story recounts the touching incidents that we meet with in every page of the Gospels.

Why do we not read every day these divinely inspired pages. Why not meditate on the countless proofs of love our sweet Lord has given us? Though we do not live in the time of Christ, though we do not look on His Divine countenance, we have the fullest, clearest chronicle of all He said and did. If we only read these pages, we will not complain that we do not see our Dear Lord.

GOD'S ESPECIAL LOVE WAS SHOWN TO SINNERS

The common fear that presents itself to most minds is that we are weak and sinful, full of faults and defects. How then can we be saints?

Our Lord, answering this objection, tells us that He came on Earth, not for the just, but for sinners. He showed His friendship for sinners so clearly that His enemies in derision called Him "the friend of sinners."

He tells us, "There shall be joy in heaven upon one sinner that doth penance, more than upon ninety-nine just who need not penance." (*Lk.* 15:7).

He assures us that if our sins are as red as scarlet He will make them as white as snow. This He is doing every day.

He chose for His Apostles sinners, rude, weak men. St. Peter denied Him; St. Thomas refused to believe in His Resurrection; all, with the exception of John, abandoned Him in His Passion. St. Paul was a fierce persecutor of the Church and sought to destroy His work.

Yet these weak and sinful men He made so strong that they glorified in suffering for Him. In the face of every danger and difficulty they divided the whole world between them, as mighty conquerors, destroying paganism with all its horrors and implanting in its place Christian civilization.

How touching was His pardon of the poor woman taken in the commission of adultery. The Jews sought to force Jesus to condemn her to a cruel death, which was the penalty established by the law for the crime that she had committed.

They pushed her, covered with shame, forward before Our Lord and denounced her.

Our Blessed Saviour said to her accusers: "Let him among you who is without sin cast the first stone at her."

Full of confusion, they slunk away.

Then Jesus said to the sinner: "Woman, has anyone condemned thee?" She replied, "No, Lord."

"Neither shall I. Go in peace. Sin no more."

She left His presence overflowing with love for Him.

This is what He says to us each time we go to Confession, but alas, we are not so grateful as she was!

How lovingly He defended Magdalen who, in the house of the proud Pharisee, kissed His feet and washed them with her tears and wiped them with her beautiful hair.

And the Pharisee who had invited Him, seeing it, spoke within himself, saying: "This man, if he were a prophet, would know surely who and what manner of woman this is that toucheth him, that she is a sinner.

"And Jesus answering, said to him, Simon, I have somewhat to say to thee. But he said: Master, say it.

"A certain creditor had two debtors, the one owed five hundred pence, and the other fifty. And whereas they had not wherewith to pay, he forgave them both. Which therefore of the two loveth him most?

"Simon answering, said: I suppose that he to whom he forgave most. And Jesus said to him: Thou hast judged rightly.

"And turning to the woman, he said unto Simon, Dost thou see this woman? I entered into thy house, thou gavest me no water for my feet; but she with tears hath washed my feet, and with her hair hath wiped them.

"Thou gavest me no kiss, but she, since she came in, hath not ceased to kiss my feet.

"My head with oil thou didst not anoint, but she with ointments hath anointed my feet.

"Wherefore I say to thee: Many sins are forgiven her, because she hath loved much . . .

"And he said to the woman, Thy faith hath made thee safe, in peace." (*Luke* 7:39–50).

OUR MANY SINS, OUR FAULTS,
OUR WEAKNESSES

Seeing then God's infinite goodness and mercy for even the greatest sinners, let us banish our foolish fears and doubts. No matter how weak we are, God's grace will make us strong. Let us have *boundless* confidence in God's mercy!

Nothing pleases Him more than to pardon us, to purify us, to give us His friendship.

Bear ever in mind His divine assurance, **"If your sins be as scarlet, they shall be made white as snow."** (*Is.* 1:18).

CHAPTER 5

The Passion

We now come to a subject that even the pen of a saint cannot sufficiently describe, *viz.*, the sufferings and death of our Sweet Lord.

Who could have imagined the possibility of God suffering, despised, crucified?

He could have saved us by one word, as He had created us. Why then did He subject Himself to such awful humiliations, such agonies of pain, to that most ignominious of deaths, meted out to only the greatest malefactors—crucified between two thieves, mocked and blasphemed by His enemies!

One drop of His Precious Blood would have saved a thousand worlds.

Why then did Our Sweet Lord suffer such pain and degradation?

Simply to prove the infinite sincerity of His love for us. And we—careless, insensible, thoughtless, blind—remain unmoved at the sight of all He did for us.

We look on our crucifix and feel no pity for our Crucified Lord. We look on the Stations of the Cross and feel no answering sorrow stir our hearts.

He did all that God could do to constrain our love, but our coldness, our incredible blindness nullifies all that His Divine Love did to gain our affection.

Worse still: "By our sins," the Apostle tells us, "we crucify again the Son of God and make a mockery of Him."

The Jews had been waiting and praying for the coming of Our Lord for 4,000 years. The Prophets, one after another, foretold the principal facts of His life. He Himself then came and worked astounding miracles to prove that He was God.

But at the sight of His sufferings, the Jews were scandalized; they could not believe that God could suffer.

The Gentiles, although they saw the wonders He wrought, were no less incredulous. They called it madness to say that God would submit to such outrages.

We know and believe that He is God, that He suffered and died for *each one* of us, yet we are more guilty than the Jews and the Gentiles, for we remain hard and ungrateful at the sight of all that Jesus has done for us.

Why do not our hearts burn with love of Him? Because we do not trouble to think on the Passion; we do not ponder on it; we do not love it.

WHAT MUST WE DO?

Clearly, we must love and honor the Passion. The following are very easy ways of doing so. We honor the Passion:

1. **By making the Sign of the Cross**. We make the Sign of the Cross very often; let us make it slowly and reverently. Made reverently, it gives great honor to God. Made hastily, it insults God and is a kind of parody of the Passion.

    Let us remember that *each* time we make the Sign of the Cross, *a*) We offer the Passion and death of Jesus Christ to the Eternal Father, *b*) We thank Our Lord for dying for us on the Cross, *c*) We offer the infinite merits of the Passion for our own souls and for the salvation of the world.

Each time we make the Sign of the Cross this way, we console the Heart of Jesus; we obtain pardon for our sins; we help to save the world from great evils.

2. **By repeating often the Holy Name of Jesus**. Because St. Paul tells us that **Jesus** merited His Name by His Passion and death. Therefore, when we say Jesus, we should have the intention of offering the Passion and death of Jesus Christ to the Eternal Father in union with all the Masses being said all over the world.

3. **By kissing our crucifix**, especially after our morning and evening prayers, and before and after saying the Rosary.

4. **By saying the Five Sorrowful Mysteries** of the Rosary, asking Our Lady to give us a great love for the Passion. We thus honor the Passion of Our Lord and the Dolors of Our Lady.

5. **By making the Way of the Cross**. The 14 Stations bring vividly before our minds the sufferings of our Saviour.

6. **An excellent and most meritorious way** of honoring the Passion is by offering all our sufferings, pains and troubles in union with the sufferings of Our Lord. This gives our sufferings an indescribable value and obtains for us strength and patience to bear them patiently.

It is so easy to say: "All for Thee, Dear Jesus, Who hast suffered so much for me."

7. **By studying the Passion**, that is, by reading some books on the Passion.

8. **Hearing and offering Mass** is the best of all means of honoring the Passion because the Mass *is* the Passion. It has the same value and brings us the same graces as the Sacrifice of Calvary did.

It is lamentable to see how few Catholics hear Mass

with this intention. During Mass many do not even think of the Passion. The Mass is not an imitation of Calvary; it is the same Sacrifice as Calvary, though in an unbloody manner.

These are all very easy ways of honoring the Passion.

WHAT THE SAINTS SAY

a) The Saints say that five minutes' prayer in honor of the Passion is of greater value than many hours spent in other devotions.

b) St. Alphonsus says that all the Saints became saints by devotion to the Passion and that there was no saint who had not a great love of the Passion.

c) Devotion to the Passion gives intense pleasure to Our Lord. Want of devotion to the Passion wounds His Sacred Heart most deeply.

d) Our Lord said to St. Bernard, "I will remit all the venial sins and I will no more think of the mortal sins of those who honor the grievous wound on My right shoulder, which caused Me unutterable pain when bearing My heavy Cross to Calvary." We honor this wound by saying the Fourth Sorrowful Mystery of the Rosary.

e) Our Lord promised St. Gertrude that He would protect, most especially in the Judgment, those who make loving reparation to Him for the insults, outrages and blasphemies heaped on Him in His Passion.

This we can do by offering to Our Lord all the offenses, slights and humiliations we may have to bear.

f) Our Lord said to St. Mechtilde: "Those who thank Me for the awful thirst I endured in My Passion I will reward as if they had assuaged My thirst on the Cross.

"And those who thank Me for having been nailed to the Cross for love of them I will reward as if they had taken Me down from the Cross."

We can do this by saying the Fifth Sorrowful Mystery of the Rosary.

CHAPTER 6

After His Ascension

Before leaving us, Our Lord promised that though in Heaven He would still be with us here below. His last words were, "My peace I leave you, My peace I give you, a peace that the world cannot give, a peace that surpasses all comprehension."

Fulfilling this promise, He has ever continued to give us proofs of His tender love. Not only does He protect His Church from her enemies, but He appears frequently to His Saints, manifesting the most intimate love for them.

We read in the life of St. Anthony how Jesus appeared to the Saint in the form of the Divine Child and most lovingly caressed him and allowed Anthony to caress Him in return.

His intimacy with St. Rose of Lima was perhaps more touching.

He appeared to her constantly, and when He delayed the hour of His visit, the Saint, who enjoyed the visible presence of her Guardian Angel, bade the Angel fly to Heaven and tell Jesus that her heart was burning with love and that she could wait no longer for His visit. The Divine Child with loving condescension came at once in answer to her message. He was wont to call her "Rose of My Heart."

St. Catherine of Siena was still more honored by Our Lord. He appeared to her frequently and recited the Divine Office with her. He took out her heart and replaced it by His own Sacred Heart, that thenceforward she might love Him, not with her heart, but with His Divine Heart.

Appearing to her on another occasion, in company of His Blessed Mother and the Saints, He made her His spouse and placed a ring on her finger, which she retained ever after.

"Catherine," He said, "think of Me and I will think of thee."

As a crowning favor, He gave her the marks of His five wounds on her hands and feet and side.

St. Agnes of Montepulciano received the most wonderful graces, even from her tenderest years, and so wise and prudent did she become that at the age of twelve she became prioress of her convent by order of the Pope.

Our Blessed Lady placed in her arms the Child Jesus, who treated her with the most intimate affection, allowing her to detach from His neck a little gold chain and medal, which she made her own.

St. Teresa of Jesus once saw the Child Jesus in her convent, who asked her: "Who are you?" The Saint replied, "I am Teresa of Jesus." "Oh! then," said Our Lord, "I am Jesus of Teresa."

We might multiply indefinitely similar incidents, did our space allow.

We mention these few to show what kind of love God has for us and what kind of love He wishes us to give to Him.

He is not content with our service, our adoration; He asks us, *above all*, for our love, He asks us to love Him with all our heart and soul, with all our strength and mind.

These proofs of love, one may urge, God gave to the Saints, but not to us. We dare not hope for such intimate proofs of love.

That is a wrong inference. He gave these proofs of love to the Saints, not only for their sakes but *to show us also* how loving, how tender He is.

HE HAS DONE EVEN GREATER THINGS FOR US

But why complain? Our Lord has given each of us proofs of love as great and greater than those visible favors just mentioned, which He gave to the Saints.

Does He not come to us *daily* in Holy Communion, if we allow Him? He, the great Creator of Heaven and Earth, comes, not into our arms or into our rooms, but into our very *souls*. He not only comes, but He comes with infinite love. He unites Himself to us so intimately that He, the great God, becomes *one with us*. Did He fold us in His arms and press us to His bosom, it would be much less than when He unites Himself to our souls in Communion.

He does not come for a moment; He stays in our souls as long as the Sacred Host retains the appearances of bread.

Strange blindness of many Catholics who receive Communion and who do not *enjoy* it!

As Martha and Mary longed for the visits of Jesus to their home in Bethany, as St. Rose longed for the visits of the Divine Child, so should we long for the visit of Jesus in Holy Communion and *enjoy* it. He is in our souls as really and truly as He is in Heaven.

What will He not give us in these precious moments if only we ask Him? He is not only in our souls, He is there with infinite love. He pours out His graces on us with infinite generosity. We eat His Flesh and drink His Blood. Our souls are bathed, purified, strengthened by this Precious Blood, the same Blood that flowed for us on Calvary.

Oh, if Christians only understood the wonders of Holy Communion, they would not complain that God has not given them as intimate, personal proofs of His love as He gave to the Saints!

The glorious Angels themselves, were they capable of jealousy, would envy us the wondrous grace of Holy Communion. These great Angels do not receive God as we do, but stand around us gazing with ineffable love as Jesus enters our hearts. As long as He remains in our souls, they adore and bless and praise Him in an ecstasy of delight. They see here something that they do not see in Heaven itself.

Oh, that we understood the unspeakable grace of Holy Communion! All Eternity will not be sufficient to thank God even for one Holy Communion.

What more could God do for us than come into our souls and make Himself one with us!

What more could He do than give us His Flesh to eat and His Blood to drink.

Holy Communion thus made will make us saints.

JESUS ON OUR ALTARS

And, as if that were not enough, He remains on the Altar, waiting for our visits, ready to console and comfort us, ready to pardon the most depraved sinner, even as He pardoned the Publican in the Temple, to give help and strength to the weak, to comfort the sad, to console the sorrowful.

This Sacrament is indeed a Sacrament of peace and love. Here Our Lord is on a throne of Mercy, continuing the work of His life on Earth, but—dare we say it—in a more merciful way.

When on Earth, He was in one land; only the people of that land could hope to approach Him. In the Blessed Eucharist, He is in all lands, in all cities and towns, even in the deserts, wherever a Catholic missionary is found.

He is really and truly present; He sees us distinctly; He hears us; He loves us. He is waiting, longing for our visits.

A few incidents of recent occurrence will show us how really Our Lord is on the Altar.

A Protestant Minister in England was taking a walk with his little daughter, six years old. They entered a Catholic Church, where the minister explained to his little girl the meaning of the Way of the Cross and other objects of note in the church.

The little one, attracted by the red lamp burning before the Tabernacle, asked what that meant. Her father replied that it was to show that Jesus was in the Tabernacle.

"Jesus!" she exclaimed. "Our Jesus, the Son of God?"

"Yes, dear."

The child was deeply impressed. Even after, when walking with her father or mother, she insisted on going into a Catholic church to see the lamp and to visit Jesus.

Wonderful visits! Our Lord was speaking to their hearts.

After six months the child with her father and mother became fervent Catholics.

In London, two girlfriends, one a Catholic and the other a Protestant, went shopping. Passing a church, the Catholic said goodbye to her friend, as she wished to assist at Benediction.

The Protestant, however, entered the church to wait. She remained standing, looking about. It was the first time she had been in a Catholic church.

When, however, the priest placed the Monstrance with the Blessed Sacrament on the Altar, she instinctively fell on her knees and folded her hands on her breast, gazing at the Sacred Host.

On leaving the church, to the surprise of her friend, she asked to be introduced to the priest. She wished to become a Catholic, though never before had she thought of it.

A Protestant young man fell in love with a Catholic girl, but after some time, as he refused to become a Catholic, she declared that she could not marry him, though she loved and respected him very much. She begged him to consider the affair ended and asked him not to write to her again.

Broken-hearted, the young man took his annual holiday and went off to a country village to try to forget his grief.

The hotel in which he stayed was near the Catholic church, and he could see from his room the Tabernacle lamp. The lamp became a fascination for him; sitting at his table, his eyes invariably turned toward it. It became an obsession.

He asked the servant who had charge of his room what that red lamp meant. Smiling, she answered, "It is the red lamp that burns before the Blessed Sacrament."

The obsession continued, and finally he resolved to enter the church and see it for himself.

On entering the church, great was his surprise to come face to face with the girl whom he had so wished to marry.

"What has brought you here?" he exclaimed. "I came," she answered, "to nurse my aunt, who is ill." "And what," she asked in turn, "brought you into this Catholic church, you who refused to think of becoming a Catholic?" He told her simply that the red lamp, which he could see from his room in the hotel, fascinated him and he had to come to see it.

"Then continue," she said, "Our Lord Himself is calling you." He did so and gradually his doubts and dislikes for the Church cleared away and he became a fervent Catholic and the happy husband of the girl he loved.

STILL ANOTHER INCIDENT

A gentleman and his wife, both staunch Protestants, had a business transaction with the priest in whose parish they lived. Unfortunately the settlement of this affair caused annoyance to both parties, and the Protestants became more embittered than ever against the Catholic Church.

Some time elapsed, and the lady happened to be passing the church. Feeling tired, she went in to rest. She remained for twenty minutes, enjoying the calm and silence and looking at the High Altar.

This visit was repeated frequently, at first merely with the wish to rest, but gradually this gave way to a feeling of pleasure and peace.

A few months passed and both husband and wife became Catholics!

If then Our Sweet Lord works so wonderfully on those souls who did not even pray to Him, what will He not do for those who pray fervently to Him?

As we get warmth and comfort when we approach a blazing fire in the wintertime, even so, our poor cold hearts are filled with the fire of love when we kneel lovingly before Jesus in the Sacrament of the Altar.

He is the same God who in Heaven fills the Angels with love. Here in the Blessed Sacrament He is on a throne of mercy and wishes to fill our poor souls with peace and joy. We are in the midst of Angels, who stand around the Altar praying with us and for us.

Our Lord has many times shown Himself in the Blessed Sacrament to help our faith.

We will mention just one fact.

Thomas of Cantimbre, the celebrated Dominican Bishop, famed for his profound learning and deep piety, describes a miracle which he himself witnessed in company with many others.

Having heard that Our Lord had appeared visibly in a consecrated Host in the Church of St. Amand in Douay, he immediately hastened thither and begged the priest to open the Tabernacle and expose the Sacred Particle. Many persons flocked to the church on learning of the Bishop's arrival and were privileged to see the miracle once more.

The Bishop tells us what he himself saw: "I saw my Lord face to face. His eyes were clear and had an expression of wondrous love. His hair was abundant and floated on His shoulders; His beard was long, His forehead broad and high; His cheeks were pale, and His head slightly inclined. At the sight of my loving Lord, my heart well-nigh burst with joy and love.

"After a little time Our Lord's face assumed an expression of profound sadness, such as it must have worn in the Passion. He was crowned with thorns and His face bathed in blood.

"On looking on the countenance of my Sweet Saviour thus changed, my heart was pierced with bitter grief; tears flowed from my eyes, and I seemed to feel the points of the thorns enter my head."

Though we do not see Our Dear Lord as the Bishop did, He is there on the Altar, the *same* loving Lord.

MY LORD AND MY GOD

Oh, how we all should like to speak to the good God, the God of peace and love, the God of infinite mercy and compassion!

We should like to speak to Him, as Peter and James and John did. We should like to gaze on Him, as did the multitudes who thronged around Him in Judea, who looked into His face, who heard the wondrous words of love that fell from His lips and sank into their hearts like a heavenly balsam.

Wonder of wonders, all this we can do if only we have a living, understanding, undoubting faith in the Blessed Sacrament.

Jesus is on the Altar as really and truly as He is in Heaven, as really and truly as He was on Earth, the self-same God of infinite mercy and love. He is waiting for us, for you and for me. Let us go in and kneel at His feet and speak to Him in the Tabernacle.

CHAPTER 7

We Must Do Everything
for the Love of God

St. Paul is the great master of the spiritual life. No one can teach us better than he how to become a saint. Here are his very words: "Whatever you do in word or work, do all in the Name of Our Lord Jesus Christ." Lest we may think that the Apostle is speaking only of offering our spiritual acts to God, he goes into particulars and says: "Whether you eat or whether you drink, or **whatever else** you do, do all for Our Lord Jesus Christ."

There are no acts more material, more necessary, than eating and drinking. Therefore, St. Paul mentions these to show us that we must do *everything* for the love of God.

Take these words, Dear Reader, as directed to yourself by the Apostle, and you have at once another great secret of sanctity.

To do this, it is not necessary to add one iota to your prayers or devotions; you have merely to form the intention of offering your every action for the love of God.

This makes your every work meritorious. All your acts give pleasure and glory to God. It does not matter whether you succeed or fail in your enterprises; your acts have the same merit.

Thus, the countless acts of every day are pleasing God and earning for us rewards for all eternity.

On the other hand, if we neglect to follow this rule of the Apostle, all our acts are worthless. We deprive ourselves of wonderful rewards, and we rob God of His glory and pleasure.

Think for a moment on the long lives of 50, 60, 70 years, every day of which is full of energy and activities—but *all are lost if we do not offer them to God!*

Do not think, Dear Reader, that what St. Paul recommends is impracticable or impossible, a thing that only Saints can do. There is no difficulty whatever in offering our acts to God, and there is nothing more consoling, nothing more meritorious.

HOW TO GIVE EVERY ACTION
THIS INESTIMABLE VALUE

The first act of every good Christian in the morning is to fall on his knees and make his Morning Offering. It can be done in this wise: "Sacred Heart of Jesus, through the most pure hands of Mary, I offer Thee all the prayers, works and sufferings, all the actions of this day and of all my life, in union with the Masses being offered all over the world, for the intentions of Thy Sacred Heart and for the Apostleship of Prayer. Every breath I draw, every beating of my heart, every glance of my eyes, every step I take, every single act I do, I wish to be an act of love for Thee."

This little act takes *one minute*, but it must be done slowly and with full deliberation. We must mean what we say. It is a short act, but it gives immense value to every action. Our every act, as a consequence, gives glory to God and receives a distinct reward in Heaven.

This offering has still more value if, from time to time during the day, we renew it by saying briefly: "All for You, dear Lord."

Who can be so foolish as to neglect this sacred obligation, yet many make the act in a careless, distracted fashion. Some do not make it at all!

All the saints and holy writers attach the gravest importance to the Morning Offering.

CHAPTER 8

The Principal Duties of the Day

We shall now consider the principal duties of the day, each in particular, and see how we may avoid the many grave faults commonly committed in their performance, and on the contrary, we shall see how we may derive from these same duties the very greatest graces.

These duties are Prayer, Work, Eating, Sleeping and Suffering.

1. PRAYER, OUR FIRST DUTY

The most important duty in our everyday life is Prayer. On it depends all our happiness. We must, therefore, form clear ideas of how to pray. Those who understand what prayer is find in it pleasure and delight.

Prayer brings us into close, intimate, personal contact with God. When we pray, Almighty God gives us all His attention. He is looking at us, hearing our every word, ready to give us everything that is good for us. He hears our every prayer. If, as sometimes happens, we ask for what is not good for us, God does not give us that.

Our prayer, however, is not lost, for in this case He gives us something else, something better. We rather gain than lose.

God is infinitely good. He loves us with a boundless love. He is our dearest Father and we are His children. Consequently He readily gives us all that can make us happy.

Moreover, He has promised in the most explicit way to hear our prayers.

"Ask and you shall receive, seek and you shall find, knock and it shall be opened to you." God never breaks His word. Yet many do not seem to believe Him! When they need something they use every possible means of getting it, except the best means of all, *viz.*, **prayer**.

Prayer is an intimate and loving talk with God. We are really and truly in His presence. It is enough to bear this clearly in mind, and then our prayer becomes an intense consolation.

As in the case of other Christian duties, the trouble about prayer is our *ignorance*. We have not been properly instructed. The great reality of prayer has not been explained to and impressed upon us.

Two things we do in prayer: We offer God our love and adoration, as the Angels do in Heaven, and we ask Him for all we need.

If God seems deaf to our prayers, it is simply because He wishes to prove our faith and confidence in Him. We must pray and pray on. St. Peter tells us that we must take Heaven by violence, for the violent bear it away. The more we pray, the more we receive. By delaying to hear our prayer, God is actually giving us more and better graces.

We have a touching example of this in the case of the poor woman of Canaan who, crying out, said: "Have mercy on me, O Lord, thou son of David: my daughter is grievously troubled by a devil.

"Who answered her not a word. And his disciples came and besought him, saying, Send her away, for she crieth after us.

"And he answering, said, I was not sent but to the sheep that are lost of the house of Israel.

"But she came and adored him, saying, Lord, help me.

"Who answering, said: 'It is not good to take the bread of the children, and to cast it to the dogs'.

"But she said: Yea, Lord; for the whelps also eat of the crumbs that fall from the table of their masters.

"Then Jesus [showing all His sweetness and love] answering, said to her, O woman, great is thy faith, be it done to thee as thou wilt: and her daughter was cured from that hour." (*Matt.* 15:22–28).

In this touching story, we see the admirable confidence and perseverance of this poor woman, a striking example for us to follow.

We also see how, not only was her daughter cured, but she herself was filled with joy and consolation.

What graces do not those receive who pray in this way, who blindly trust in the goodness of God and who storm His Sacred Heart!

2. OUR DAILY PRAYERS

Our first and most important prayer is the Morning Offering. Immediately on arising, we should fall on our knees and make this offering, slowly and deliberately, as already explained above.

Morning and evening prayers are most important factors in human life. Far from being a matter of minor importance, they are the most urgent of our daily obligations. If well said, they obtain for us all needful graces and protect us from the many evils that may be awaiting us in the course of the day.

If badly said or omitted, we expose ourselves to grievous calamities. Many fall victims to disease or are killed by accidents or meet with premature deaths because they had not prayed.

There is certainly one peril that we have to face every day of our lives, which comes, as St. Peter and St. Paul warn us, from the fearful malice of the devil, who is ever using his keen angelic intelligence to work our ruin. We are as defenseless as children in his hands. Woe to us if we have not God's help in this daily conflict with our implacable enemy! That infallible help is obtained by prayer.

Many Catholics seem to have little fear of the devil. They take no precautions against his attacks. He is the greatest evil and the most terrible danger that menaces us during *all* our life and most especially at the hour of death. For this last moment he reserves his most awful attack.

He hates us with a malignant hate, for we are destined to occupy the glorious throne in Heaven which he has lost. This thought lashes him into fury. He has made a careful study of us and knows our every weakness; he notes our evil inclinations and when we are off our guard, as a result of having omitted our prayers, he redoubles his temptations.

Many fall in this unequal combat, and if death surprises them in this state, they are plunged into Hell for all eternity.

Such is the oft-recurring story of thousands of lost souls. This fact alone should be enough to make us careful in saying our daily prayers well.

But there is a far more powerful incentive to make us love prayer, and this is that our prayers are the expression of our filial love for our dear Heavenly Father, they are our loving homage and adoration to our Creator.

Morning prayers as found in prayerbooks are five, *viz.*, the Our Father, the Hail Mary, the Apostles' Creed, the Confiteor and Hail Holy Queen.

At night we add to these a short examination of conscience with a fervent Act of Contrition.

Had we the misfortune to fall into mortal sin, we must redouble our contrition and go to Confession as soon as possible.

By mortal sin we expel God from our souls and give His place to the devil.

These prayers must be said slowly, reverently, on our knees and in our bedroom. In this room we spend a third part of our lives, and here we shall probably die. Therefore, it is well to sanctify it by our daily prayers.

The Rosary. All good Christians say the Rosary *daily*, thereby insuring the most special protection of God's Holy Mother, which she promises to those who daily say her favorite prayer. Devotion to Our Lady is looked on by the Saints as a sure guarantee of our eternal salvation.

The Popes, the Bishops of the entire world, priests in every country, all the Religious Orders have been urging the faithful for the past 700 years to say the Rosary.

The Saints not only recommended it, but said it themselves with unspeakable devotion and confidence.

Why this universal and extraordinary love for the Rosary? Because by it we deliver ourselves from every danger and obtain every grace and blessing.

God's sweet Mother has come in recent years to Fatima to preach the Rosary as the easiest and most certain way of saving the world from the dire calamities that are threatening it.

Millions and tens of millions of men and women, hearkening to her message, are sending up their daily pleas for mercy.

Woe to the foolhardy Christian who turns a deaf ear to this message of salvation!

The Catholic homes where the Rosary is said by the members of the family are visibly protected by God.

Daily Mass and Communion. Better than the most lengthy prayers and the severest penances, the surest of all means of becoming holy is by assisting at daily Mass and receiving Holy Communion.

The Mass is Calvary here again; it has the same infinite value and brings us the same oceans of graces as Our Lord's death on Mount Calvary.

Our Lord offered His sufferings and death for each one of us in particular. In the Mass He mystically dies again for each of those who assist at the Holy Sacrifice.

One Mass gives Him more glory than the praise and adoration of all the Angels and Saints in Heaven.

Multitudes of Angels stand around the priest and offer our prayers to God.

The blessings and favors we receive at *each* Mass we hear are indescribably great.

How foolish are those who can assist at Mass and are too lazy and negligent to do so!

We have already spoken of the consolations and joys we receive in Holy Communion. (See page 39). No one who pauses to think on these will refuse to receive God daily into his heart. Only crass ignorance can explain such negligence.

The Name of Jesus. An easy practice that we urge our readers to adopt is to form the habit of repeating frequently the Holy Name of Jesus. Each time we say, **"Jesus,"** we offer the

Eternal Father all the infinite merits of the Passion of Jesus Christ, in union with the Masses being said all over the world. We thus participate in these thousands of Masses. There is no devotion so easy, none so infallible in obtaining for us God's richest graces.

It demands no time, for we can repeat the Holy Name hundreds and even thousands of times in the day—when dressing in the morning, when working, when walking, in our homes, in the streets, everywhere.

This practice gradually fills our hearts with peace and happiness; it delivers us from many evils and obtains for us more graces in a single day than we may otherwise hope to receive in a whole year.

Devotion to the Sacred Heart is a very certain way of becoming holy; our sweet Lord Himself gave it to us as His last, supreme effort to gain our love.

To practice this devotion we must:

a) Read from time to time the 12 wonderful Promises that Our Lord made to **everyone** who practices devotion to His Sacred Heart. (See page 96 at the end of the book.) These Promises reveal in the clearest possible way the immense personal and tender love Our Lord has for us. Therefore, we should read them, slowly and carefully, at least on the First Friday of every month. They will awaken in our hearts boundless confidence in Our Lord.

All the 12 Promises are most important, but we call attention very especially to the 11th Promise: *"Those who spread this devotion will have their names written on My Sacred Heart, never to be effaced!"*

We can spread the devotion by talking of it to friends, by distributing little pictures of the Sacred Heart with the Promises printed on them.

b) We must repeat frequently the ejaculation: "Sacred Heart of Jesus, I have confidence in Thee, boundless confidence for everything."

This ejaculation is so powerful and efficacious that it has been well called *"The miraculous ejaculation."*

c) We must wear a badge or medal of the Sacred Heart.

d) We ought to have a picture of the Sacred Heart, not only in our homes but in every room and on our writing table, just as we have the photograph of our dear mother. We can say from time to time, "Jesus, I love You."

No mother, no father, no brother or friend loves us so tenderly as Jesus does.

Those who practice devotion to the Sacred Heart in this simple and easy way have a guarantee of receiving the wonderful favors promised by Our Lord.

These daily prayers and devotions will make us saints. They are:

The Morning Offering.
Morning Prayers.
Evening Prayers.
The Rosary.
The frequent repetition of the Holy Name.
Devotion to the Sacred Heart.
Daily Mass and Communion.
A visit to the Blessed Sacrament.

3. WORKING

Most men work seven, eight, ten hours a day, and some even more. This goes on for fifty, sixty or even seventy years. All these countless hours are, for many, completely lost! Also, work for some is irksome, especially when it does not bring in the desired profits. Others enjoy their work but never think of doing it for God, and they too lose the immense merits of all these long hours.

Everyone should bear in mind that work was expressly imposed on us by God as a penance for sin. "In the sweat of thy face shalt thou eat bread." (*Gen.* 3:19).

If we work in this spirit, every moment of labor is a meritorious penance. And when our work is not successful, we have the great consolation of knowing that it brings us a still greater reward because of the mortification resulting from our failure.

In our Morning Offering we should be careful to emphasize the words, "I offer *all the work, all the actions* of this day for the intentions of the Sacred Heart."

Few Christians feel inclined to practice penance for their many sins. Consequently, their pains in Purgatory will be long and severe. If, however, we offer our life's work, the work of every day, its weariness, worries and disappointments, we are doing excellent penance, the holiest we can perform, because it has been imposed by God Himself and we are doing it every day of our lives.

Moreover, our work, our every action, if done for God, will receive abundant rewards because they are acts of love.

All these innumerable graces are utterly lost if we fail to do our work with the proper dispositions, *viz., a)* as acts of penance, *b)* as acts of love.

By making our Morning Offering with full deliberation, the countless acts of each day become acts of merit.

4. EATING

This is another all-important duty of our lives, one too which ought to inspire us with gratitude to God for the abundant and good food He gives us. Alas, eating is a duty which for many is not only devoid of merit but the occasion of many sins!

We should commence our meals by saying the usual short grace: *"Bless us, O Lord, and these Thy gifts which we are about to receive from Thy bounty, through Christ Our Lord. Amen,"* asking God to bless us and the food and drink which we are about to consume. This blessing will certainly please God and give our food an additional nutritive value.

On one occasion wicked men sought to kill St. Benedict by offering him a glass of poisoned wine The Saint, as was his wont, made the Sign of the Cross over the wine before tasting it; whereupon, the glass was shattered into pieces and the malice of his false friends made manifest.

Doctors assure us that much illness is caused by eating too much, by eating too hastily, and by eating what is not good for us. Many commit these faults, which are injurious to both soul and body.

A safe rule to follow is to arise from table before being fully satisfied, but rather with an inclination to eat more.

Mr. Gladstone at the age of 80 declared that he attributed his great age and splendid health to the fact that he ate slowly, and carefully masticated his food.

Eminent doctors advise their patients to observe carefully what foods agree best with them and what are likely to do them harm, choosing the former and avoiding the latter. Those who follow this sage advice will enjoy good health and save themselves from many sins.

SOME ADDITIONAL HINTS

We are reminded by the bread we take and the meat we eat of the Heavenly Bread we have received so often in Holy Communion, and of the Flesh of Jesus Christ which we have eaten at the Sacred Table.

This thought is a beautiful Spiritual Communion.

TWO LITTLE PRAYERS

"O My God, I offer Thee this act in union with Jesus Christ, in the power of the Holy Spirit and in praise of Thine Eternal Majesty."

This prayer, Our Lord assured St. Gertrude, gives indescribable value to any act we perform.

"O my God, I offer Thee the awful thirst Jesus Christ suffered in the Passion, His fast in the desert, His Divine moderation during His life on Earth."

This prayer obtains pardon for any want of abstemiousness and for any gluttony in eating and drinking we may be guilty of.

Let us be content with the food which is placed before us.

St. Paul's words must be before our minds: *"Whether you eat or drink, or whatsoever else you do, do all to the glory of God."* (*1 Cor.* 10:31).

We should not be unchristian in showing our dislike or discontent when our food is not just to our liking. If there is something very wrong with what is placed before us, then we may call attention to it courteously. We must eat as intelligent beings, not as animals.

5. SLEEPING

We devote 7 or 8 hours a day to sleep, that is a third part of our lives. Few Christians derive from their rest the merit they might easily obtain. These 7 or 8 hours of every day are for many *lost hours*, and in some cases the occasion of sins of slothfulness.

What a pity to lose 8 hours every day! Some sleep too little, some too much, some yield to excessive laziness in arising.

The following suggestions will enable us to transform these 8 hour's sleep into 8 hours of prayer and merit.

a) Our sleep is a sacred duty imposed on us by God, and its fulfillment ought to be an act *of obedience* to God.

b) We ought to say our night prayers slowly and devoutly, asking for a good night's rest.

c) Let us offer our sleep to Our Lord in union with His sleep during His life on Earth. Bear in mind that every action united to the acts of Our Lord has an indescribable value. Priests, before beginning their Office, unite it with the prayer of Jesus when on Earth.

d) Let us offer every breath we draw, every beating of our hearts during the night as so many acts of love for God. **Thousands of acts of love every night!**

e) Our dear Angel Guardian is with us all night, watching over us, just as a tender mother watches over her sick child. Say a few loving words to this dear Angel before closing your eyes.

f) Good Christians sprinkle holy water every night over their persons and bed as defense against the devil.

g) If we cannot sleep, let us offer this weariness in honor of the three hours Jesus Christ passed on the hard bed of the Cross. Let us go on repeating the Name of **Jesus**, and this will help us to get the desired rest.

h) Regarding rising, we ought to form the habit of getting up *immediately* when our clock strikes or when we are called. The habit of jumping up quickly makes rising more easy. Laziness or delay in getting up makes it more difficult. It is also a bad beginning for the day, a beginning claimed by the devil.

i) When dressing, we should accustom ourselves to repeat frequently the Holy Name of **Jesus**. These first moments of the day are most precious, and we should offer them to God. This habit will guarantee us the help and protection of God during all the day.

An amusing fact is told of a young woman who was rather lazy and slow in getting up. On being called one morning she turned over again and said, "I am tired this morning; I will sleep a bit longer." She heard a voice, as of one lying beside her, which said, "Do, do, and I will remain with you."

Recognizing the devil, she bounded from her bed and was never again inclined to sloth when arising.

We may well apply this fact to ourselves, for it is quite certain that if we are lazy and slothful, the devil is really beside us and snatches the first fruits of the day from God.

How many thousand Catholics could easily hear Holy Mass and receive its indescribable graces if they were less lazy in getting up!

Frequently, too, laziness in arising makes us hurry over our morning prayers or even neglect them entirely. This is a very grave fault and may cause disastrous consequences. No one should dare to omit or say hurriedly his morning prayers.

6. THE PROBLEM OF LIFE

Suffering is thought by many to be the *great evil* of life. Oh, if they could only avoid it!

If they did find a way of avoiding it, *that* would be the greatest evil of their lives.

All about suffering. Our Lord has given us a most perfect redemption. He could have dispensed the law of suffering if He so willed. Why does God, being of infinite goodness and mercy, ask us to suffer?

For the simple reason that suffering is a very great grace.

Our suffering is a share, a small but most valuable share, in the Passion of Our Dear Lord.

It is priceless in value—if we only accept it and offer it in union with Christ's Passion.

He has suffered unspeakable agonies for each one of us. Are we such arrant cowards as to refuse to suffer a little for Him?

How little gratitude we show for all that He has done for us! The easiest and best way of thanking Him is to offer our daily crosses and trials for love of Him.

The one big trouble about suffering is that we do not know *how* to suffer. We have no idea of its merits.

The secret is to suffer with patience and serenity. Then suffering loses all its sting, all its bitterness.

If we only remember that it is Our Sweet Lord Himself who asks us to bear these daily trials for love of Him, suffering loses its horrors.

God gives us abundant strength and grace to bear our crosses, if we ask Him.

Many good and pious Christians never think of asking God to help them to bear their crosses! Therefore, their crosses weigh heavily on them.

Our sufferings are the purest gold in our lives. Five minutes' suffering is of greater worth than twenty years of pleasure and happiness.

The Son of God suffered, His Immaculate Mother suffered, the Apostles, the Saints, all God's friends suffered. Suffering therefore must be a great grace.

One of the most lamentable evils in our human lives is that we lose the immense rewards which our sufferings ought to merit.

We fear suffering, we hate it, we revolt. It is not the suffering, but this revolt, that makes suffering unbearable and makes us cross, irritable, peevish. On the other hand, suffering borne patiently brings out all the beautiful traits of our character. It refines us as fire purifies and refines gold.

One fact well worth remembering is that our daily sufferings, the least as well as the greatest, if borne well, merit for us a crown of martyrdom.

A second is that the priceless graces and rewards which our sufferings should bring us **are lost** if suffering is borne badly.

Consequently, let us remember this about suffering:

1) That it is our share of the Passion of Jesus Christ; therefore, it has indescribable merit.
2) That, if borne with patience for the love of God, it loses all its sting and bitterness.
3) That if we ask God, He will most certainly give us abundant strength to bear the sufferings He sends us.
4) Our sufferings will save us from the fearful pains of Purgatory.
5) **Suffering, well borne, makes us saints.**

CHAPTER 9

Reading

Another easy and effective way of arriving at an eminent degree of holiness is **spiritual reading**.

We have pointed out that the reason for so little sanctity in many souls is not weakness or malice, but *ignorance*. Spiritual reading dispels this ignorance and helps us to feel all the charm and consolation of God's blessed love.

Every Catholic should without fail make spiritual reading daily for ten or fifteen minutes. The neglect of this duty is disastrous.

To derive benefit from our reading, we must observe the following rules, which will not only secure satisfactory results but will make our reading attractive and a real pleasure.

Read books that appeal to you. It is of elementary prudence to choose proper books, for not every good and excellent book suits all readers.

It must be our aim to find a book or books that make an appeal to *us personally*, that will grip our attention and act as a driving force, a stimulant to our energies.

Pray before reading. Next, it is well to say a short prayer, one Hail Mary, before commencing our reading, asking Our Blessed Lady to help us to understand what we are reading and to put it into practice. St. Thomas Aquinas told his fellow Dominican, Father Reginald, that he got his great treasures of knowledge more by prayer than by study.

Read your book not once but many times. It is a fatal mistake to read a book quickly or to read it only once. That produces very little good. We must not read a spiritual book as we read a romance. However well-written a book may be, the *truths* it presents are so great that our poor weak minds only succeed in grasping them little by little.

It may treat of the first of all truths, *viz.*, the *love of God*. Nothing seems easier to understand than **that**, yet daily experience shows how very vaguely and insufficiently this wonderful doctrine is grasped and, as a consequence, how very little God is loved.

One book read slowly does us more good than a hundred read hurriedly.

One fact, one conversation, one little story has often changed the whole tenor of a man's life. The following incidents related to the writer by a dear old priest show that even what appears at first sight trivial may exercise a lasting impression on one's conduct.

"When a student in college," he told me, "my confessor kindly gave me some advice one day in recreation. It seemed simplicity itself, yet that advice has given me the most profound consolation all the long years of my life and has moreover enabled me to give similar consolation to the souls of many who have consulted me.

"A second incident was my hearing a short story about the Mass some months after my ordination. This left a vivid and indelible impression on me so that I have never celebrated the

Holy Sacrifice without thinking of it, and as a result I enjoy deep devotion in saying every Mass."

A third fact which this good priest mentioned is no less surprising.

"A lady friend of mine once said to me, 'I confess that I feel no special sympathy for your young curate One thing, however, that he does impresses me very much. When he passes in front of the Altar of the Blessed Sacrament, he genuflects so reverently and looks with such devotion at the Tabernacle that it would seem as if he saw God.' This remark was made to me thirty years ago, and never once since then have I myself passed in front of the Blessed Sacrament without imitating the example of my curate. This has given me a notable increase of faith in the Real Presence."

If then a short conversation, a little story, a few words of advice can make such a deep impression on one's mind, a book is likely to make much more, for it may contain scores of such facts.

THE POWER OF A GOOD BOOK

St. Augustine was one of the greatest geniuses that ever lived. Unfortunately, he was plunged for many years in error and vice. One of the chief means which made him a great saint was the reading of a good book, the life of St. Antony of the Desert.

St. Ignatius was a rough soldier, trained in the camp and not given much to piety, yet by reading one book he became the great saint that he is. He himself has written a book, *The*

Spiritual Exercises, which has converted and sanctified thousands of its readers.

St. John Columbini was a very lax and indifferent Christian. Dinner was delayed one day, and he became very irritated. His wife offered him a book to amuse him until such time as dinner was served. Glancing at the title and seeing that it was a pious book, he flung it on the floor in a fury. Regretting this insult to his wife, he picked it up sat down and began to read it.

So great was the impression it made on him that he changed his whole life and became a saint.

La Harpe taught the most impious doctrines, which he published in books very cleverly written, causing great harm to his readers.

He was thrown into prison, where the solitude proved almost intolerable. He found a pious book, which though far from his liking, he read for amusement.

Gradually, he became engrossed in it and read chapter after chapter. He was completely converted.

On leaving the prison, he dedicated the rest of his life to writing charming books, in a noble effort to undo all the mischief he had formerly done.

One of the gravest problems that defied the ablest American statesmen for many years was abolition of slavery. Congress after Congress, Administration after Administration came and went in the effort to help the unfortunate slaves.

Finally, a lady writer published a book, the story of a poor slave, which aroused the indignation of all who read it. This book made it feasible for the government to abolish slavery forever in the United States and to set free the millions of slaves who were held in cruel bondage.

A good book that appeals to us is the best and most powerful of preachers. It enlightens us, it stimulates us, it consoles us. We ourselves see every day the wonderful results obtained by the reading of even short, pithy pamphlets.

A celebrated London barrister, himself a convert, distributes small pamphlets, leaving them in trams and trains, on benches in the parks or streets. By this means he has done considerable good.

We shall mention one case. Returning home after a busy day, he put one of these leaflets on a railing in front of a house. A Protestant policeman seeing it, put it in his pocket and went home.

As a result of reading it, he and all his family became fervent Catholics.

Frank Estis, a young American officer, wounded in the War, found the long hours in bed so tiresome that he asked his friends to bring him something to read. They brought Catholic magazines, which were eagerly read, not only by Frank but by all the men in the hospital ward. At the end of eight months, he was able to count on many conversions of Protestants and lapsed Catholics!

On leaving the hospital, he and some others began to visit the hospitals, prisons of the city, the houses of the poor, and they now count hundreds of conversions **every year**.

It is then sheer madness for Catholics not to give ten or fifteen minutes **every** day to reading some good book.

No one should dare to dispense himself from this imperative duty. St. Dominic, great saint as he was, though constantly preaching, and spending whole nights in prayer, yet found time to read assiduously the lives of the Saints.

St. Thomas of Aquinas, a prodigy of learning and sanctity, did likewise and found his delights in such reading.

And so, too, did all the Saints.

Good reading is so pleasant and easy a way of reaching an eminent degree of sanctity that it commends itself to everyone.

BOOKS THAT WE RECOMMEND

The E.D.M. series of books are eminently suited to help their readers to grasp the great truths of our holy Religion in an easy and practical way. They are warmly recommended by Cardinals, Archbishops and Bishops.

If read in the manner we have just explained, they will prove a wonderful help and stimulus in the spiritual life.

"How to Be Happy—How to Be Holy"

This work has some excellent pages on prayer. Hosts of readers declare that by reading them they have learned to pray as they never prayed before. Prayer has become a pleasure to them. They feel that they are speaking to God.

This book explains each of our daily prayers, throwing a flood of light on them, which gives the prayers a completely new value.

Many Catholics repeat these prayers without even thinking of the words, much less of their meaning!

This book, too, gives a beautiful and thrilling account of the *Rosary*, a story utterly unknown to most of those who are saying the Rosary every day of their lives.

It gives an admirable explanation of the Mass which every Catholic would do well to read. It shows how the graces we receive even in one Mass exceed anything we can imagine.

His Grace the Archbishop of Evora says, "This book is a veritable manual of piety, eminently practical and suitable to all readers."

His Grace the Archbishop of Aveiro: "When reading this book the soul of the reader is insensibly filled with a feeling of piety and with an earnest wish and desire to be holy. The thoughts are at once elevated and practical, sublime and yet simple."

His Lordship the Bishop of Guarda: "This book is worthy of all praise. It is splendid and, if carefully read, will be a powerful help to us in the accomplishment of all our duties."

"The Wonders of the Holy Name"

This is what the Mercier Press has to say of *The Wonders of the Holy Name*.

"This little booklet, *The Wonders of the Holy Name*, is one which every Catholic should read. The average well-instructed Catholic will find much in this book to *astonish* him regarding the enormous efficacy of the simple repetition of the Holy Name and the abundance of graces and blessings which flow from its recital."

Packed into this little work are an explanation of the doctrine of the Holy Name, of its meaning and how to use it.

Then follows a collection of the most wonderful stories of delivery from wars and plagues by its recitation, of miracles performed by the Saints through its power. It is a book most timely for our troubled era.

This booklet is warmly recommended by Cardinals, Archbishops and Bishops. More than 300,000 copies have been sold in a short time.

"All About the Angels"

"This book on the Angels comes at a most opportune moment, for no better remedy can be found for the suffering in the world at the present moment than the all-powerful protection of God's Angels.

"The Angels are our best friends, and you tell your readers all about them in a way so full and interesting that your book will awaken a great love and confidence in these glorious Princes of Heaven. In return they will obtain for us many graces and deliver us from great evils."

✠ *Peter Ciriaci,* Apostolic Nuncio Lisbin

"Accept my warmest thanks for your precious book on the Angels. It is most interesting and opportune Give us more books of this kind, which will bring comfort, truth and consolation to all."

✠ *Anthony,* Archbishop of Braga

"All About the Angels is a book so full of charm and delight that it is with a feeling of regret we reach the last page and find that there is nothing more to read."

✠ *John Evangelist,* Archbishop Bishop of Aveiro

The Catholic Voice says: "Written with the object of spreading a devotion *largely unknown* even among good practicing Catholics, this book on the Angels introduces us to new and startling revelations about the great power and love for us of those glorious beings.

"Supported by facts and irrefutable proofs, the book reads like a fairy tale.

"It is a book that will charm all, priests and people young and old.

"It is certainly one of the most beautiful books on the Angels yet published.

"Above all, this book on the Angels does all who read it **one incalculably great benefit;** it makes them know and love their Angel Guardian, whom so many ignore as if he did not exist! Yet he is their most loving, most powerful, dearest friend. He has done them countless favours, for which they have never thanked him! He will do them still greater favours if they only know and love him. They want *happiness;* he will make them happy."

"The Land of the Eucharist"
A thrilling story of old Portugal. Its every page is full of interest.

"Read Me or Rue It"
"This booklet fully deserves its title. It puts before its readers the great doctrine of Purgatory in a striking way, quoting as authorities the great Saints and Doctors of the Church. It grips the attention from the start and takes a message straight to the heart."

—R. F.

"How to Avoid Purgatory"
"It is not too much to say that these pages will confer an inestimable benefit on those who peruse them with attention.

"The author gives clear and weighty reasons to show that it is quite possible to avoid Purgatory. Best of all, the means he points out to attain this end are well within the reach of all devout Catholics."

—F. D.

"St. Patrick and the Irish"

"A little work that will fill the heart of every lover of Ireland with a great and just joy."

—A. M.

These books form most attractive reading and are very inexpensive, as they are intended for mass distribution. If your Catholic book shop does not stock them, write to the publisher for a copy of those titles currently available.

CHAPTER 10

Meditation

We here deal with the most important subject of our lives, *viz.*, **daily meditation**.

Many Catholics do not even know that they are bound to meditate!

Our Lord Himself tells us why so few become holy, why so few become saints. "The whole world," He says, "is gone astray because no one thinks in his heart." Remark the words of Our Lord, "No one thinks in his heart," that is, no one bothers to understand, to realize, to grasp in all their fullness the wonderful, the most consoling truths of our Religion. Willful blindness!

As we have already said, God has given us a most lovely Religion, which He made expressly to help us, to console us, to make us happy. It is not a difficult Religion, made only for saints. It was made for us, poor sinners, to strengthen our poor weak natures, to console these hearts of ours which are thirsting for peace and happiness. This Religion, if only properly understood, will help us to overcome all our sins, all our defects, and it will make us solidly happy and really holy.

How is it that we do not understand this? Simply because we neglect our great duty of daily meditation, and therefore our ideas are vague and hazy and of little or no use to us. One clear idea is worth a thousand hazy ones.

The easiest and best way—the only way—to have clear ideas is to make a short daily meditation.

Meditation does not consist in thinking all the time. We read a little, think a little, and make short little acts, as we shall now explain. Nothing is easier.

WHY MUST WE MAKE MEDITATION

First of all, *every Catholic* should make daily meditation. St. Teresa says that the person who does not meditate needs no devil to throw him into Hell; he is going there himself.

Second. Meditation is by no means hard to make, if only we learn how to make it, and this presents no difficulty.

Third. If we do not meditate, we never see our faults, and so we never correct them.

Fourth. If we do not meditate, we can form no idea of the malice of sin, and as a consequence, we do not feel sorry for it; we do not avoid it.

Fifth. If we do not meditate, we do not see the *awful* danger we are in of falling into Hell. For this reason, thousands of men and women—men and women like ourselves—are falling into Hell *every* day.

Sixth. If we do not meditate, we do not prepare for death; we are afraid of death; we are afraid to think of it. That is just the reason why so many have bad deaths. Those who know how to meditate on death are no longer afraid of it, and moreover, they are sure to have happy deaths. "Think of your last end and you shall never sin," are God's own words.

Seventh. The greatest happiness anyone can have on this earth is to have a good friend, a true friend, a friend who can and is ready to help him.

God is really and truly our Friend in the truest sense of that word. He is our most loving Father, a most tender Father.

Never was there a father or mother on this Earth who loved a child as God loves us. The day we understand this truth will be the happiest day of our lives.

We must always think of God as a God of tenderest love. Then we must love Him.

The only reason why we do not love God is that we do not meditate; we do not see how good God is; we do not pray to God to help us to love Him.

If we do not meditate, we shall never see how good, how sweet God is; we shall never be holy, and we shall never be happy.

Why do so few go to daily Mass? Mass has exactly the same value as the Death of Christ on Mount Calvary. Why do they not go frequently to Holy Communion, which is the greatest grace God can give them?

Why do they not enjoy Holy Communion?

Why do they not visit God in the Blessed Sacrament, though they pass the open door of the church so often, perhaps many times a day?

They lose all these helps, all these consolations, all the strength, all the happiness God offers them simply because they do not make daily meditation.

Meditation is *so important* that nothing can take its place.

It is not in itself as holy an act as Mass or Holy Communion, but it is *more important* because we cannot hear Mass properly nor receive Holy Communion devoutly unless we meditate. We cannot pray as we should; in fact, we can do nothing well unless we meditate. All the vocal prayers we can say will not take the place of meditation.

Everyone must banish the thought that meditation is difficult or disagreeable. That is the great temptation of the devil and is an utterly false idea.

We repeat that meditation is easy, is pleasant and brings us graces and blessings that we otherwise shall never get. **Every Catholic is bound to meditate.**

AN EASY WAY TO MEDITATE

Here is a simple and easy method of meditation, which all may use with advantage.

a) As we said when speaking of reading, we must choose for the purpose of meditation a book that we like, that suits us, that has a personal appeal to us. Each one chooses the book he likes best.

b) We begin our meditation by praying to the Holy Spirit for light and guidance. For ordinary Christians a very easy and beautiful prayer to the Holy Spirit is the Third Glorious Mystery of the Rosary. This in itself is a little meditation. We see how timid, how fearful the Apostles were, how rude, how slow in understanding Our Lord's teaching; above all how weak they were even after Christ's Resurrection. They remained ten days waiting and praying for the coming of the Holy Spirit. They had the doors closed in fear of the Jews.

Then the Holy Spirit descended on them, resting in the form of fiery tongues over their heads and gave them all His gifts and graces.

They were completely changed. No longer afraid, they went into the midst of their enemies and preached Jesus, the Son of God, whom these had crucified. They were no longer rude and ignorant, but full of wisdom and knowledge. They confounded the philosophers of Greece and Rome, they feared neither sufferings nor tortures, and were even pleased to suffer for the Name of Jesus.

These men who had been so timid, so rude, so weak were now able to convert the world.

This lesson is most encouraging, for we see what we too can do with the help of God, no matter how weak we are.

c) After saying this Mystery fervently, let us take up our book and read a little—slowly, carefully, attentively, turning over in our minds the meaning of what we have read, applying the lesson to ourselves. Then we pray, asking God to help us to understand what we have read.

Again we read a little, and pray a little, a second, a third time, each time applying the truth to ourselves.

d) Then we make a practical resolution, which we must bear in mind during the day.

e) Lastly, we must pray fervently to God to pardon our past faults and give us strength to avoid them in the future. What could be easier?

THE RESULTS OF MEDITATION

Meditation is like a kind and good friend who teaches us, advises us, encourages us.

This friend is in reality the Holy Ghost, who enlightens our understanding and strengthens our wills and gives us His graces and gifts, as He gave them to the Apostles.

We see our defects and humbly ask God to pardon us. We consider God's love and earnestly ask Him to make us love Him more and more. We see how blind we have been in the past regarding the truths of our Holy Religion. We beg the Holy Spirit to help us to understand Our Dear Lord's wonderful teaching.

Meditation made in this way is very easy and of the greatest importance. It is a grave obligation. Only those who are very ignorant are excused from meditation.

SUGGESTIONS

In order to aid those who wish to meditate, we shall now suggest some thoughts on a few important subjects that may help them. Remember what has been said: "Read a little, think a little, pray a little, apply the truths to yourself, make your resolution."

THOUGHTS ON PRAYER

Prayer is the greatest power in the world, even the prayer of the ordinary Christian.

Few, very few know how to pray, and yet it is so easy. Because they do not know how to pray, they are losing immense graces, immense blessings every day.

Thousands are going to Hell every day because they do not pray. Thousands and thousands are sad and unfortunate because they do not know how to pray.

Our morning and evening prayers, if well said, save us from countless evils and obtain for us countless blessings. Many Catholics have not the faintest idea of the *immense* importance of these prayers.

They have many pressing occupations, but the gravest of all their duties, the most important and urgent work of the day is morning and evening prayer. As a result of these prayers, God Himself and His Blessed Mother bless and protect us.

PRAYER IS A PLEASURE

Few enjoy prayer, for the same reason: that they have never learned to pray.

The first thing we must understand *clearly* is that when praying we are talking to God personally, intimately, really. God is looking at us, giving us all His attention, ready to give us all we need.

What an immense joy and consolation it is to realize that we are talking to God Himself. But so many pray as if they were gramophones, talking machines, not even thinking of the words they are saying.

Many say their prayers in haste! That surely is not speaking to God.

St. Augustine says that God prefers the barking of dogs to prayers said hastily.

We must pray intelligently, slowly, thinking of what we are saying. Then our prayer is a pleasure, for we know that it is pleasing to God and that it is bringing us great graces.

The writer had once a long private audience with Pope [St.] Pius X. He was all alone with the Pope in his private room. The Holy Father was most gracious and kind and gave him all he asked for and even more.

Yet we have a private audience with God whenever we pray. We are all alone with Him, and He is infinitely sweet and merciful. But how few enjoy this intimate, personal converse with God.

If they understood that they were *actually* speaking to God, they would not think it a penance to pray; they would not be so easily distracted.

The Arabs give us a lesson in prayer. When they pray to Allah, they are so wrapt up in their prayer that they think of nothing else. In fact, frequently their enemies, knowing this, choose the moment they are praying to rush on them and kill them.

GOD HEARS EVERY PRAYER

Still another most consoling thing about prayer is that God hears every prayer. Every prayer well said, as any ordinary Christian can say it, brings us back a great grace, a favor, though we may not see it.

True, God does not always give us exactly what we ask, because He sees that it would not be good for us, but then He gives us something better, which He knows *is* good for us.

Good businessmen, wise statesmen, great generals, place all their trust in prayer.

THREE CONDITIONS OF PRAYER

We must *persevere* in prayer; we must storm Heaven as the Apostle tells us.

We must pray with the *fullest confidence*, for the greater our confidence, the greater will be the graces we receive.

We must pray *with humility*. God loves the humble and gives them what they ask in rich abundance.

THOUGHTS ON THE LOVE OF GOD

There is nothing that makes us so happy as to love God.

To love God is the greatest work of our lives.

We are made expressly to love God. Every act of the love of God is of priceless value and will have an eternal reward.

One act of love is worth a thousand acts of any other virtue, just as one little diamond is worth a thousand gold pounds. On the other hand, everything else we do, even if we were to do mighty things, if we were to spend fifty years in some great work, all is worth nothing, nothing, if we do not do it for the love of God.

Does that mean that all the work, all the occupations of every day during all our lives are worth nothing?

By no means. Everything we do, every occupation, every employment, resting, sleeping, eating, enjoying ourselves, all will have merit, if we only do them for love of God, because God wishes it.

God made us to work, God commands us to sleep and to eat. Therefore, we can and should do everything for love of God.

Surely there is nothing more easy.

That is just what St. Paul tells us: "Whatever you do, in word or work, whether you eat or whether you drink, do all in the name of Our Lord Jesus Christ."

That is what good Christians do when they get up in the morning. They kneel down and make their morning offering: "Sacred Heart of Jesus, I offer Thee, through the pure hands of Mary, all the prayers, the works, the sufferings of this day, in union with the Masses being offered up all over the world, for the love of the Sacred Heart and for the Apostleship of Prayer."

This simple prayer makes every act of the day an act of the love of God. All the better if during the day we sometimes confirm it by saying, "All for Thee, Jesus."

The morning offering takes only one minute, but we must say it *deliberately, slowly, meaning* what we say.

To love God, is very easy, if we only remember how infinitely good He is. He has given us everything we have, He has made us like Himself, to His own image and likeness. He has made us not as servants but as His own children, who will be with Him forever in Heaven, seated on thrones like the Angels, enjoying His own immense happiness.

With immense love He suffered and died to save us. Then He mystically dies for us *every* day in the Mass and offers up His sufferings and death for us. Every Mass has exactly the same value as the death of Our Lord on Calvary! Can it be possible?

He is in the Blessed Sacrament in every Catholic church in the world. He is there as really and truly as He is in Heaven.

He is waiting for our visits. We can get oceans of grace if we only visit Our Lord in the Blessed Sacrament. And yet how few visit Him!

What more could God do for us, what more could He give us?

He is our best, our dearest, our most loving Father, and He commands us to call Him by this loving name, "Our Father, Who art in Heaven."

All the mothers and fathers of the whole Earth do not love us so tenderly, so really, as our sweet Lord does.

If we only meditate on all this, we must love God.

But also, in all our prayers, our first, most important, our principal intention should be to ask God for His love, more love, more love.

There is nothing He gives us more readily, more abundantly, than His blessed love.

We all desire to have a good friend, a friend who really loves us and is always ready to help us.

A man loves his wife and she him, and this is their greatest happiness.

A mother loves her children. There is no love on Earth so wonderful as the love of a mother.

But God's love for us is more real, more true and gives us more happiness than all the love of wives and husbands and friends and mothers.

To think that the great God of Heaven loves me with infinite love—tender, personal love!

THOUGHTS ON PATIENCE

Everyone can be patient, no matter how excitable he may be by temperament. Some of the Saints who were most notable for their sweetness were naturally excitable, nervous and bad-tempered, as for instance, St. Francis de Sales.

How to be patient. Let us see how patient people are happy. One goes to purchase things in a shop where the owner is patient and affable, but we avoid a shop where the clerks are irascible.

Among those whom we know, the best loved are those who are kind and patient.

When visiting the sick, we notice how those who are patient suffer relatively little. The impatient ones intensify their pains a thousand times.

Walking in a crowded street, if we observe the passersby, we see some that are hasty, disagreeable, rude; whereas others are calm and dignified.

This should serve as a daily lesson for us, a daily reminder.

Doctors tell us that impatient and excitable people suffer very much from heart troubles and brain troubles and shorten their lives considerably, even by many years.

Everyone who wishes to be happy, to be loved, to have a long life, should make *every effort* to be calm and patient and should ask God fervently in all his prayers to make him patient.

Our Lord tells us, "Learn of Me to be meek and humble of heart, and you shall find peace to your souls."

Each day let us try anew to be patient, and still *more* patient. If we live with disagreeable people, who offend and even insult us, we must take no notice of them. Let us only think of ourselves.

Three rules: Never speak when you are angry. Never lift your voice. Never say a disagreeable word.

In the home an impatient person is a devil. He is unhappy himself; he makes others unhappy; he commits countless sins.

A patient person is an angel, is loved by everyone, is happy himself and is loved by God.

CONFESSION

Confession is one of the greatest and easiest of all means that God has given us to become Saints.

Why did Our Lord come on earth? **Why** did He live with us for 33 years? **Why** did He suffer and die?

To save us from sin, to help us to sin no more.

Surely then, He left us some especial and all-powerful means to overcome sin and temptation. That means is *Confession*.

Yet many Catholics have a most erroneous idea of Confession. They look on it as something hard and distasteful; whereas, God meant it to be a divine help to overcome our weakness, our inclinations to evil. He meant it to be an immense consolation in all our troubles and trials.

This is most certainly true for all those who take the trouble to understand it.

The writer has met many Protestants who seem to understand Confession much better than Catholics. Many Protestant men asked him to hear their confessions and were sorely disappointed when he told them that he could not do so. Several began at once to prepare to enter the Catholic Church, simply to be able to go to Confession!

One gentleman asked to be received into the Church, and when asked why, he replied, "Because I want to be able to go to Confession. We have nothing in our church that helps and consoles us as Confession consoles Catholics." And he became a staunch Catholic.

We see that very many Protestants in late years go to confession to their Protestant divines!

But why confess to a priest, to a man like ourselves?

Because God in His infinite sweetness saw how much our human hearts seek comfort, and therefore, by an act of infinite power and wisdom, He has given men this divine, omnipotent power of pardoning sin and comforting, consoling and helping sinners to become good. He not only gives them His own Divine Power to forgive sin, but He also gives them the light and wisdom necessary to console and counsel poor sinners.

EVERY DAY WE SEE THE
WONDERS OF CONFESSION

A poor boy who is tempted to steal confesses his fault, and the priest at once shows him not only the meanness and malice of stealing, but shows him how dangerous it is to him. If he is discovered, his character is ruined for life. He is branded as a thief. That boy never steals again.

A young girl is tempted to go astray, attracted by some foolish young man. A word from the priest opens her eyes and her honor is saved.

A husband or a wife begins to be unfaithful; they confess it, and once more the confessor, with a timely warning, saves the poor family from ruin.

A servant confesses that he or she has taken the master's money. Again, a few kind words make them honest and loyal forever after.

Doctors, lawyers, judges confess negligence in their duties; the wise counsel of the priest makes them serious and upright.

How many Protestants have been surprised on receiving money from a priest—sometimes large sums—which had been stolen from them and which the priest was asked to restore.

Many Protestant families choose Catholic servants, but servants who go to Confession!

For any right-minded man, Confession represents not only a personal benefit, but a safeguard for society.

In the last Great Wars, the power of Confession was shown in a wonderful way on the battlefields. One of the great English Protestant newspapers used these words: "The Catholic soldiers, when they have their chaplains, fear neither man nor the devil."

The number of Catholic chaplains in the English army in the beginning of the First World War was 36. It was increased to 600, and this by a Protestant government!

THE POWER OF FORGIVING SINS

No one but God can pardon sin. Even the highest Angel in Heaven cannot absolve from a single sin. God by an act of infinite power and mercy has given priests this divine power.

St. Alphonsus says that if Our Lord Jesus Christ were to sit in one confessional and a simple priest in another, the sinners who went to the priest would be as fully pardoned as those who had confessed to Christ.

St. Augustine declares that when a priest absolves from sin he uses a power greater than the power used by God in creating the world! In proportion to this Divine Power are the benefits we receive in Confession.

THE GRACES OF CONFESSION

Confession, like the other Sacraments, is a river of divine grace, which flows from the heart of God into the heart of the sinner.

What is grace? Few understand and appreciate this divine gift, and yet it is the most wonderful reality in our lives. St. Peter tells us that it is a real participation in the divine nature, raising us up, ennobling us, strengthening, purifying and beautifying our souls, making us like the angels, likening us to God Himself. It gives us a completely new life, a new vigor, a new power. It gives a divine light to our understanding, by which we grasp the divine truths which God has revealed to us, which otherwise we could never understand.

It gives a new and mighty energy to our wills so that we can perform all our duties well and easily.

But Confession has its own **special** graces. Dear reader, weigh them well:

First of all, it pardons our sins. Secondly, it gives us light to see the enormity of sin. Thirdly, it gives us strength to avoid sin. Fourthly, it is the easiest and best penance we can perform because it washes our souls in the Precious Blood of Jesus. It thus lessens our time in Purgatory, or possibly delivers us altogether from Purgatory. Fifthly, it comforts and consoles us, most effectively. Sixthly, it makes us love God and hate sin. Seventhly, it helps us potently to correct our defects, which make us so disagreeable to others, make us so unhappy ourselves and make us offend God.

We are weak. It gives us a new strength and life, so that a person who falls constantly into great sins and cannot avoid them, will be certainly able to avoid them if he goes to Confession frequently.

Priests are seeing this every day.

All men long for a good friend, whose friendship and love they enjoy, to whom they can go in their troubles and difficulties and ask for advice. A good friend is one of the greatest blessings God can give us.

Confession gives us this friend, for in Confession we meet a man who is there expressly to help and console us. He has been prepared especially for this work by long years of training. He is kind and helpful.

We may open our hearts to him, sure that he will understand us and sure that he is competent to give us the best possible advice.

We are equally certain that he will keep absolutely secret all that we say to him. A priest never breaks faith with his penitents.

WHAT MUST WE DO TO
GET ALL THESE GRACES?

Confession is very easy, but it is, as we saw, very holy, very wonderful, a divine Sacrament. Therefore, we must make a short but *fervent* preparation. The reason why so many confessions do so little good is that Catholics do not make this fervent preparation.

To go to Confession without a serious preparation is to tempt God and profane this most holy Sacrament. Confession is easy, but we must treat it with respect. God tells us that He does not cast His pearls before swine. These words are very strong, but very true.

We must pray fervently, by saying, for instance, the first three Sorrowful Mysteries of the Rosary, or we may say the prayers we find in our prayerbook.

Then we make a careful examination of conscience, that we may see and be able to confess our faults clearly and briefly.

The most important part of our preparation is to excite ourselves to sorrow, **real sorrow**, for our sins and make a firm resolution to avoid all mortal sins, and as far as we can, venial sins, especially any notable venial sin.

If we are not sincerely sorry for our sins, and if we are not firmly resolved to avoid sins, we are insulting God when we go to Confession.

HOW CAN WE HAVE THIS
REAL SORROW FOR SIN?

By clearly understanding the horrible malice of sin.

Sin is a deliberate offense against God. No man will do wrong if he sees a policeman looking at him. But we know clearly that God is looking at us, and still we deliberately offend Him; we offend Him to His very face.

The fire of Purgatory is the same terrible fire as the fire of Hell. We may be kept in this awful fire for many years for a deliberate venial sin. God could never punish us too severely. He does not send us to Purgatory because He is angry with us, but because the malice of a deliberate venial sin is simply awful—mortal sin much more so.

The Saints say there is nothing so terrible on this earth as a deliberate sin. Were we to see a dead body in horrible corruption, it would be nothing in comparison with even a venial sin.

Were a soul to enter Heaven with one venial sin, it would willingly give up Heaven's happiness and plunge itself into the awful fires of Purgatory to wash out that filthy stain.

St. Paul says that by our sins we crucify again and make a mockery of God.

By absolution we are pardoned, delivered from all the filth and corruption of sin.

Therefore, we must make sure to be really sorry for our sins, for not even the Precious Blood of Jesus applied to our souls will purify us unless we are sorry and **firmly** resolved to sin no more.

IN CONFESSION

In Confession we ask the priest's blessing and confess our sins clearly, briefly and frankly.

Then we listen carefully to any advice which the priest gives us and resolve to do exactly what he tells us.

We may ask any questions we think fit, or explain any difficulty we may have.

Lastly, when the priest is giving us absolution, we must say our Act of Contrition fervently, just as if we were at the feet of Jesus Christ Himself.

AFTER CONFESSION

After Confession, we must thank God for the wonderful graces He has given us; we must say our penance with all our heart. He has pardoned our sins, no matter how grave and horrible they were. It is simply incredible how few Catholics thank God as they ought to do for the wonderful graces received in Confession. It is the story of the ten lepers over again.

APPENDIX*

HOW TO GO TO CONFESSION

Examine your conscience.

Be sorry for your sins and make up your mind not to sin again (at least not to commit mortal sin again).

(Kneel down, make the Sign of the Cross and say . . .)

"Bless me, Father, for I have sinned. It has been _____ days (weeks, months, years) since my last Confession. I said my penance and went to Holy Communion. I confess to Almighty God and to you, Father, that I have . . ."

(Here tell all the mortal sins you may have committed since your last good Confession, and the number of times you committed them, and then, if possible, tell the number and kind of your venial sins. Then say . . .)

"I am sorry for these and all the sins of my past life, and I ask pardon of God and penance of you, Father."

(Listen to what the priest says, and especially note the penance he gives you. Then say an Act of Contrition.*)*

The priest will give you absolution and finish by saying words such as, "God bless you. Go in peace."

After leaving the confessional, say or perform the penance the priest assigned you.

---

*Added by the Publisher to the 1990 edition.

An Act of Contrition

O my God, I am heartily sorry for having offended Thee. And I detest all my sins because I dread the loss of Heaven and the pains of Hell, but most of all because they offend Thee, my God, who art all good and deserving of all my love. I firmly resolve, with the help of Thy grace, to confess my sins, to do penance, and to amend my life. Amen.

THE TWELVE PROMISES OF THE SACRED HEART TO ST. MARGARET MARY
For those who practice devotion
to the Sacred Heart of Jesus

1. I will give them all the graces necessary for their state of life.
2. I will give peace in their families.
3. I will console them in all their troubles.
4. They shall find in My Heart an assured refuge during life and especially at the hour of death.
5. I will pour abundant blessings on all their undertakings.
6. Sinners shall find in My Heart the source and infinite ocean of mercy.
7. Tepid souls shall become fervent.
8. Fervent souls shall speedily rise to great perfection.
9. I will bless the homes in which the image of My Sacred Heart shall be exposed and honored.
10. I will give to priests the power to touch the most hardened hearts.
11. Those who propagate this devotion shall have their name written in My Heart, and it shall never be effaced.
12. The all-powerful love of My Heart will grant to all those who shall receive Communion on the First Friday of

nine consecutive months the grace of final repentance;
they shall not die under My displeasure, nor without receiving their Sacraments; My Heart shall be their assured
refuge at that last hour.